Scuba
Diving

William Koelzer

CHILTON BOOK COMPANY

Radnor, Pennsylvania

Scuba
Diving
how
to
get
started

Manufactured in the United States of America

Designed by Adrianne Onderdonk Dudden

LIBRARY OF CONGRESS CATALOGING IN PUBLICATION DATA

Koelzer, William.
  Scuba diving:how to get started.

  1. Skin diving. I. Title.
GV840.S78K63 1976   797.2'3   76-1000
ISBN 0-8019-6371-0
ISBN 0-8019-6372-9 pbk.
234567890   432109876

*To Gloria, Werner Erhard,
Cochrane Chase and Joe Ziemian.
They pointed the way.*

Acknowledgments

Writing a scuba book and scuba diving itself are somewhat alike in that both activities are lonely and dangerous when done alone. Fortunately, this book was written and illustrated with the assistance of a few generous, talented persons, many of whom are my frequent diving companions.

Besides teaching me to dive a few years ago, scuba instructor and photographer Robert Leite, took the underwater pictures and gave freely many hours of his valuable time. Jon Hardy, 20-year scuba veteran and nationally-recognized expert on modern diving instruction, kindly helped edit out counter-productive material and added the depth of his broad experience.

Also, thoroughly editing the manuscript were Randy Stoltenberg, AMF Swimaster; Bruce Anderson, Healthways; Grady Fort, U.S. Divers; and Harold Boehm, longtime diving companion.

Skillfully performing for the book's photos were divers Kathy Cully, Harold Boehm, and Bill and Barb Steiner. Helping, too, were Carol Raymond, Judy Leite, Pat Anderson and my wife, Gloria.

A special thanks goes to individuals at various scuba manufacturing firms who helped provide necessary gear, photos and drawings for the book, and much valuable advice: Art Stanfield and Bill Oliver of AMF Swimaster; Dell Price and Dick Smith of AMF Voit; Gordon McLaymont, Grady Fort and C. J. Wharton of U.S. Divers; and Roy Romano and Bruce Anderson of Healthways.

For her weekends, lunch hours, and long evenings of typing numerous manuscript drafts, my special thanks also to Rochelle Battermann, who incidentally, completed a scuba certification course shortly after being first exposed to diving through her work on this book, and to Stephanie Thal who suffered through typing my cryptically handwritten first draft.

Finally, my appreciation to Werner Erhard. He gave me the space to take responsibility for how this book came out, and triggered me getting clear on the real meaning of purpose.

Contents

6 Snorkeling—The Basic Skills   57

7 Water Entries   90

8 Surface Dives   98

9 Review of Precourse Training   102

10 Choosing Proper Instruction   105

11 Summary   113

Introduction

If you've always wondered just what scuba diving was all about, or if you've decided to learn how, this book teaches you the right way to get started.

If you're already a diver and simply want to let your friends and relatives know more about diving or maybe even find out how they can join you underwater, this book helps you do just that.

It explodes the common myths about sharks, a high scuba fatality rate, the need for bulging muscles, the cost of equipment, and gruelling qualification tests. It shows that diving is truly quite a safe sport—safe, providing you use your head a lot before, during, and after your basic training under an instructor's guidance.

Much of the text emphasizes a logical step-by-step precourse training guide which can help you more easily qualify for scuba course entry. This alone gives you a great headstart on what otherwise can be for some a very challenging physical and mental experience.

SCUBA DIVING: How to Get Started helps you select the very best scuba instructor and training in your area for the least amount of money. It also outlines how to choose quality diving equipment, what it costs, how to use it, and how to avoid making errors in equipment purchases. Highlighted throughout is a relatively new boon to more comfortable and safer diving—the bouyancy compensator. Photos and explanations clarify how this invention has expanded the range of diving for everyone, making it a less strenuous and far safer sport than ever before.

More than a hundred photos teach you how to get your body in shape for diving and familiarize you with basic snorkel diving gear: mask, snorkel, fins, and buoyancy compensator.

Dozens of underwater and poolside shots are carefully designed to bring you progressively towards the goal of every good, smart sport diver . . . TO BE COMFORTABLE IN THE WATER. Those words are continually emphasized throughout the text because they may be the most important words you'll ever read anywhere about intelligent diving.

Unless you must honestly disqualify yourself for physical or mental reasons, there is an excellent chance you can *bring yourself* to qualify for, and successfully complete a scuba diving course. This book alone, however, will not teach you scuba diving. In fact, it specifically avoids attempting to do so. Instead, unlike some very excellent scuba textbooks, this book is simply for use *before* a course is begun.

Maybe you've thought a lot about taking up scuba diving but have done nothing about it. Well, this book tells you what you can do right now; it also has a lot more that will help you later become a good, smart, safe, comfortable diver. The title says it all. This is simply about *SCUBA DIVING: How to Get Started.*

1
Why
Scuba
Dive?

The Trend Towards Individual Sports

We have recorded more data about the surface of other planets and the moon than about the oceans on our own earth. But with technological advances in underwater exploration techniques and improved equipment, knowledge of this largely unexplored habitat is slowly but steadily expanding. This is because none of us can look for long at something intriguing or beautiful without wanting to know more about it or possess it. And we have been looking at, and sailing over the surface of our oceans long enough. Now we are striving to understand the depths of their mysteries, fear them less, and, in fact, BECOME MORE COMFORTABLE in their foreign environments.

Diving brings you freedom, thrills, and challenge. And maybe another chance to find out something more about yourself.

Every year, over 200,000 persons complete training courses and become certified scuba divers.

The divable waters of the world offer us a challenge. A chance to prove something to ourselves and, perhaps, to someone else. Maybe it's the small brush with the unknown which diving offers, or maybe it's the desire to do something which only about one out of a hundred persons will ever do. In any case, diving is a primary example of us competing against ourselves. And that is the ultimate, most satisfying competition.

Diving is an individual sport. You do your utmost to excel at what you do and you enjoy it because, like skiing, it is you alone. And you grade each performance against a previous one.

In this country there is a renewed emphasis upon the *individual* performance. It's why a television beer commercial advises you that because you only go around once in life you should grab all the gusto you can. It's like the mountain climber standing on the paramount height, or the long distance swimmer finally touching land. Being good at an individual sport is personally rewarding.

In schools across the country, individual sport is taking its place alongside team sports. Young people seek their own identities by "doing their own thing." As part of this picture, more and more scuba classes are offered in high schools and colleges. The classes are offered because the demand is there. In 1974 alone, over 235,000 new divers were certified through school courses as well as YMCA and other officially recognized training. From 1950 to 1970, approximately one million persons became divers, yet this twenty year total was actually exceeded in the period from 1970 through 1975. The number of trained divers in the United States is calculated to be over two million. Of these, some half-million are considered *active* divers.

What Diving Teaches You

Diving teaches you much about self-reliance and using acquired skills to your own advantage. Ultimately, it makes you more confident in many other areas of life as well as diving. There is, however, a great danger in becoming *too confident* after you become a diver. Overconfidence leads to overexertion, impulsive thinking, taking chances, or violating safe diving rules learned in a basic scuba class. In diving there is perhaps only one greater mistake than becoming overconfident. And that is being unfortunate enough to have chosen poor basic scuba instruction, to avoid that, see Chapter 10.

Once good instruction is completed and you are an officially certified scuba diver, you begin learning the most important lessons diving teaches you as an individual sport. First, you learn self-control under initial stress. Then, after ten to twenty dives you start to learn the real key to a lifetime of diving enjoyment. You'll learn finally to be COMFORTABLE IN THE WATER!

What Better Buddy?

There are a dozen or more basic safety rules of diving, but any scuba instructor will tell you rule number one is *Never Dive Alone.* During and after training you should always have a "buddy" for maximum enjoyment both in sharing underwater beauty and experiences and, primarily, for safety.

Scuba diving is so rewarding from a visual and totally sensual standpoint that after nearly every dive, most divers hit the surface shouting, "Hey! Did you see that . . . ?" It could be anything from the friendly 300-pound grouper that moved to within five feet of you to the ¾" pelagic crab which you photographed with a close-up lens. Or maybe it was the sleek seal that fluttered its big eyelashes only inches from your face, then literally swam circles around you during the entire dive. Perhaps it was the thrill of finding pieces of high grade iron ore in the hold of a long-sunken wooden sailing ship in Lake Superior's Munising Bay. Or it could have been the logging era junkyards you combed through while diving shallow lakes around Winchester, Wisconsin.

Maybe it was spotting an incredible *four foot* Great Northern Pike streaking toward a chub minnow while you were diving murky Little Bay De Noc in northern Michigan. Perhaps it was the big, aggressive beaver that easily convinced you to quit poking your head up inside its family lodge. Or the bright green moray eel you hovered above as it pursued an elusive ink-spewing octopus off Diamond Head in Hawaii.

The point is, no matter where you dive in the world, you'll always continue to break the surface with your buddy and have good reason to say, "Hey! Did you see that . . . ?"

Learning from Diving's Unique Society

No matter how many years a person dives, he can always learn something new about himself or his underwater environment. Maybe that's why a group of divers chatting together on a boat, bus, plane, or anywhere noticeably form such a quick camaraderie. They instinctively realize the importance of relying upon one another not just for safety reasons in the water but also because through conversation they can learn more about marine life, new places to dive, the location of little-known wrecks, or an exciting new piece of diving gear.

Even a novice diver, just recently out of a basic course, is welcomed by veterans of the sport. In fact, experienced divers delight in answering the dozens of basic questions a novice will ask. The experienced diver probably remembers his own many apprehensions when he first entered the sport and, because of this, relates strongly and positively to the emotional and educational needs of the novice.

The reason for pointing this out is that it might seem that, as in some sports, there would exist a "pecking order" among divers who are assembled for whatever purpose. For the sake of the reader who may be concerned about this possibility, let me state that typically no such pecking order exists. Yes, there are differences in skill among divers once they're in the water, and this is easily noticed after a few years of diving. But out of the water, everyone puts on scuba gear basically the same way. The only major exception to this standard of equality is that very subtly, the more experienced divers will generally keep a watchful eye on a pair of novice divers whenever possible. Knowledge of this trait among veteran divers becomes comforting to a beginner once he becomes aware of it after a few dives.

One of the most valuable questions to ask a diver if you're not already one yourself is, "Why do you like diving?" Don't worry about ever getting only a one-liner answer to this question. For a minimum of ten minutes you'll receive a skilled "sales pitch." In fact, if you're not sure about whether you'd really enjoy taking up the sport of diving, ask experienced divers about it. You can find them at any dive shop or your local oceanside, lakes or quarries.

Don't worry about their serious expressions and "frog-man" appearance, with its associated wartime implications. They're people interested in seeing the sport expand, they want to gain converts. Few divers won't be glad to give you a complete rundown on the many items of gear they wear or what they saw on the last dive.

Best of all, if you show how interested you really are, you'll probably receive the name of a local instructor to call or dive store to visit. And that's good, because if that diver and his friends mutually recommend an instructor and dive store, chances are they will be good choices for you, too.

2 Exploding Scuba Myths

Misconceptions

Over two million people are trained as divers in the United States. This is about one out of every one hundred persons; of these about 25 percent live in California, with Florida now almost equalling that percentage.

Despite this lack of a large diving population, interest and awareness of diving increases whenever a diver drowns or a shark makes a rare attack. In the entire history of scuba diving in the United States, only several deaths have been attributed to sharks. In such cases there is sometimes a great, though temporary, interest in diving. This, however, is usually negative publicity and due more to uninformed newspaper reporters than to any genuine public interest in what's happening to divers. Apart from these rare occurrences, ask yourself when is the last time you read an objective, indepth newspaper article on the sport of scuba diving?

Little real understanding exists about diving among the general public. As a result, certain misconceptions have persisted since the early 1950s when the scuba system was first introduced to the United States by Captain Jacques Cousteau. This misunderstanding, however, is easy to comprehend since the sea was then, and still remains, largely a *mysterious* place for exploration. The public believes it to be a place filled with dangerous marine life such as sharks, sting rays, electric eels, killer whales, barracuda, salt water crocodiles, sea snakes, collapsing sunken wrecks, treacherous rip currents, giant squid, and the like.

Sharks

It also seems there are an excessive number of television specials and movies featuring scuba divers inside cages against which great white sharks bang with teeth-filled jaws until a hazardous, emergency escape is required by the caged-in actor-divers. The truth is that, typically, a film crew must "chum" sharks for many hours or days with barrels of animal blood or chopped fish in order to attract the great numbers usually present for the camera. Then once the sharks have arrived, the "chumming" process is *continued* until the creatures enter a most natural feeding frenzy which offers dramatic movie footage for the producer.

Let me point out that such aggressive behavior is not always natural for a great white shark, and especially uncommon among most other sharks *unless* such an excessive degree of artificial stimulation is provided. But the myth persists that sharks are bloodthirsty manhunters of the deep, constantly a real threat to any scuba diver. This is pure bunk but is nonetheless a popular belief.

Televised dramatizations must necessarily hold viewer interest. If scuba-oriented T.V. specials and an occasional series showed divers simply swimming lazily along, pausing to pick up this or that, few people would watch the program for long. So, the dramatists show the shark attack or the giant sea clam which grasps the diver's leg 'til his air runs out. In fact, a giant sea clam closes its shell very slowly and seldom has it open enough to allow a diver's foot to enter accidently.

Sharks are, at best, unpredictable. That is to say that, statistically, rarely does a shark bite a man or woman. Since the incidence of death by shark attack among scuba divers is so small it would seem that danger from shark attack is highly overrated. The danger from sharks, then, is far less than we are conditioned by the media to believe.

Most scuba deaths are the result of unsafe practices, poor judgment, carelessness, or panic on the part of the diver. Within these categories are exhaustion, poor physical or mental conditioning, drug and alcohol use and lack of sleep—the things avoided by a prudent diver. Despite such potential hazards, out of 1,685,923 possible divers in 1973, only 118 had fatalities. Yet diving is still mistakenly considered a very dangerous sport by the public.

The Public's Awe of Scuba Divers

Perhaps because most of the public has limited contact with scuba divers, many of the uninitiated have an awe of someone who dons strange equipment and actually disappears far below the water's surface for a long time. Observers ask themselves, "What if the diver's air runs out?

What if he gets tangled up and can't free himself? What if his equipment fails while he's way down? That's scary! I could never do that."

But you can! Once you correctly learn how. Later in this book, you'll learn exercises which will help you better prepare yourself for formal scuba training.

A diver can avoid trouble provided he has had proper instruction, uses good common sense, avoids exhaustion and, most of all, learns to be COMFORTABLE IN THE WATER.

What if Everything Fails at Once?

If I were 100 feet down and all my life support gear suddenly, somehow failed, I would survive and reach the surface in a relatively relaxed state as any well trained, experienced diver would do. The mere thought of being 100 feet under water and suddenly lacking air is terrifying to most persons. That thought was also terrifying to me before my training showed there was absolutely no cause for concern. Two very qualified instructors in my basic and advanced scuba instruction courses simulated for me potentially hazardous situations which they expected me to overcome. At first, simple problems were presented in the comforting, warm water of a swimming pool. Later more complex problems were presented in open, clear water off Catalina Island and Monterey, California.

The exercises were repeated many times throughout my instruction until problem-solving became instinctive. Thus, there soon became no real emergencies, only various situations which triggered the immediate response, "I know what to do." Once the proper response was made, the "emergency" ceased to exist. It will be the same for you.

Safety. Diving Versus Flying

The required high degree of conditioning one's reflexes is not widely known among nondivers, thus there persists the public awe of the "Frogman." Actually, flying a plane requires far more understanding of equipment use, technique, and emergency procedures. Yet, we seem to believe flying is far easier to master and safer than diving. Is flying more dangerous than diving? Statistically, at least, it would seem so. In 1973 there were 1412 private airplane fatalities and only 118 scuba-related deaths. Yet most believe scuba is the more dangerous sport. This is not the case *providing* you're willing to dive *only* after proper scuba instruction and proper physical and mental conditioning.

Sport diving is dangerous only when you exceed your personal margins of safety (See Chapter 9). Bob Leite, N.A.U.I. instructor #1324, a diver since age 15, suits down after a descent. Leite is also a scuba photographer, and his underwater photos appear throughout this book.

Shallow Diving Versus Deep Diving

Despite what you've seen of divers on T.V., most real-life divers are by comparison very easygoing fellows. What they usually do is swim leisurely along the bottom in about 30 feet of water, mostly observing fish, coral, and other marine life. Actually, the best diving is done in ten to fifteen feet of water. This is because sunlight can penetrate to this depth with minimal loss from reflection and diffusion, which simply means one can see more items of interest and see them in their true vivid colors. As you dive deeper, the water absorbs color very quickly until at about 100 feet, the sea bottom appears grey. But why go that deep at all?

Sometimes, even divers who should know better think that going *deep* is a badge of courage or proof to nondiving friends of scuba prowess. Smart divers know better. They know the 10–30 foot depths are best. But if some *divers* think deep diving is the mark of a real scuba expert, how can we expect an uninformed public to think any differently? The answer is that part of the reason scuba divers are so esteemed is that they *can* go deep into the ocean and sometimes *actually do* make deep dives. But most sport divers do not.

Sport diving is far removed from the scientific or research-oriented diving seen on T.V. A good diver seldom even exerts himself to the point of heavy breathing. When a smart sport diver finds he's starting to breathe hard, he'll stop and rest, either on the surface or underwater. And that is the beauty of diving. You can be 30 feet underwater and rest, while being virtually weightless, any time you want. The same holds true when a diver is on the surface. He can *always* stop to rest, and does rest, quite frequently. Divers on T.V. never seem to rest. That's because they rested while the underwater cameras weren't running. When you first start diving, you'll rest a lot and your instructor will encourage you to do so.

In fact, some of the very best instructors I know have their students take rest breaks often during exercises even if it's apparent to the instructor that no one actually needs a rest. This is done simply to condition the students to remember the important rule: REST *until you're breathing regularly again.* Getting tired while sport diving is just plain stupid.

3 The Buoyancy Compensator

Brain Versus Brawn

There was a time a few years ago when a scuba diver was thought of as being a hulking fellow with a thick neck, heavy biceps, huge thighs, and unlimited endurance. He was also thought to be rather slow-witted. Perhaps this is because, in general, very good muscular development and high intelligence are normally not believed to be complementary.

To some degree this public impression of a musclebound scuba diver was true as recently as the early 1960s. Then a relatively new piece of equipment came into popular use and brains became far more important than raw strength, though proper physical conditioning is still an extremely important prerequisite for safe diving.

This new device had a number of different names at first: safety vest, flotation vest, and life vest. Among divers, the more sophisticated device is usually called a "buoyancy compensator" and a less sophisticated version a "vest." The terms are used interchangeably, here.

On the surface the vest is inflated so that it buoys up a diver and allows him to rest without treading water. This is particularly valuable during long surface swims, when you are heading back to a dive boat or a beach. With a vest fully inflated, a diver gains from 15 to over 50 pounds of buoyancy, depending on the vest's air capacity. You would gain about 50 pounds of buoyancy from sitting atop a closed fish net containing six inflated basketballs. If you've ever tried pushing a beach ball a few feet below the surface of a swimming pool, you'll realize that even several pounds of air is sufficient to help you float quite comfortably with most of your head above the water.

The buoyancy compensator (BC) fits around the neck, the main air compartment is located over one's chest and stomach. It is secured by a number of strong, adjustable straps so that it cannot come off in an emergency, even when fully inflated. Most are equipped with an automatic purge valve which releases just enough air to keep the vest from bursting when it is near maximum volume or when the internal pressure is a few pounds greater than the external pressure.

Dozens of good brands of BC's are available today. Nearly all major full-line manufacturers of scuba gear offer several very good vests—typically the more expensive ones. As a rule of thumb, a quality vest is the one your scuba instructor will advise you to buy, so long as it has several key features, which will be described later on.

It is primarily this piece of gear, the buoyancy compensator, which has somewhat reduced the need for bulging muscles and superhuman endurance among scuba divers. Because this air bag allows one to rest so comfortably while diving, many new divers can now enjoy the sport, limited only by a frank appraisal of his or her own physical limitations. Some, depending on their degree of physical conditioning, might be wise to dive only in very calm, clear water and range only a few dozen yards from a beach or boat. Others, in better shape, may extend their range to greater distances. But all divers, even those in the

Buoyancy compensators come in many sizes and styles. Bill Steiner's medium-volume vest from AMF Swimaster is dwarfed by Carol Raymond's new large-volume model from U.S. Divers.

best condition, have gained an *extension* of their individual abilities due to the BC.

An Expanded Margin of Comfort and Safety

The BC, classified only in recent years as being as basic a piece of scuba gear as an air tank by all certifying organizations, significantly reduces diving fatigue while one is underwater. And it offers an extra margin of safety.

Typically, at the beginning of a dive, scuba divers swim face down from a beach or boat, breathing through their snorkels to reach a given point of descent which is usually anywhere from a few to 100 yards from the beach or boat. It's common for the vest to be partially inflated beneath the diver during this time. Such inflation slightly lifts the chest so the lungs won't be so compressed by surrounding water pressure, thus making breathing easier. The vest will typically be only *partially* inflated during a snorkel swim because *full* inflation and its resultant bulk increases water drag, making surface swimming more difficult. Experience eventually teaches the proper level of inflation.

Once a snorkel swim is completed, it's a good idea to inflate the vest a little more and rest for a few moments at the surface before descending. This rest allows a diver to observe the area below in which he'll dive, plus set compass directions and discuss any final matters concerning the dive with his buddy. This will be their last chance to communicate verbally, since once underwater, they'll have to rely upon standard diver's hand signals, pantomime, or underwater writing paper (which they may carry in the pocket of their BC).

Aids to Understanding Buoyancy

From the standpoint of physics, buoyancy can be understood by familiarity with Archimedes' Principle and several basic laws governing the behavior of gases. In your scuba course you'll be expected to know these laws and precisely how they affect your body and equipment when diving.

These laws, which are listed below, are quoted exactly as they are presented in the appendix of the *Sport Diver Manual*, published in 1975, by Jeppesen Sanderson, Inc., Denver, Colorado. The *Sport Diver Manual* is a popular textbook frequently recommended by scuba instructors to their students. You can buy a copy at your local dive shop or ask your scuba instructor how to obtain the text and its accompanying workbook. Study of the Jeppesen volume, combined with your practice of the exercises outlined in this book, should prepare you extremely well for your scuba certification course.

One caution: Under no circumstances should you ever don and use scuba gear, even in a pool, unless a scuba instructor is present or you've already become a certified diver. Reading a textbook is not enough to prepare you for scuba use. You need an instructor to teach you diving. Trying to teach yourself how to use equipment is deadly.

The physical laws relating to buoyancy are:

Archimedes' Principle: Any object wholly or partially immersed in a liquid is buoyed up by a force equal to the weight of the liquid displaced. (a) A negatively buoyant body sinks in a fluid because the weight of the fluid it displaces is less than the weight of the body. (b) A neutrally buoyant submerged body remains in equilibrium, neither rising nor sinking, because the weight of the fluid it displaces is exactly equal to its own weight. (c) A positively buoyant submerged body weighs less than the volume of liquid it displaces. It will rise and float with part of its volume above the surface. A floating body displaces its own weight of a liquid.

Boyle's Law: If the temperature is kept constant, the volume of a gas will vary inversely as the ABSOLUTE pressure while the density will vary directly as the pressure. Since the pressure and volume of a gas are inversely related— the higher the pressure, the smaller the volume, and vice versa. The formula for Boyle's Law is:

$PV = C$

Where P = absolute pressure
   V = volume
   C = a constant

Charles's Law: If the pressure is kept constant, the volume of a gas will vary directly as the ABSOLUTE temperature. The amount of change in either volume or pressure is directly related to the change in absolute pressure. For example, if absolute temperature is doubled, then either the volume or the pressure is also doubled. The formula for Charles's Law is:

$$PV = RT \text{ or } \frac{PV + R}{T}$$

Where P = absolute pressure
   V = volume
   T = absolute temperature
   R = a universal constant for all gases

General Gas Law: Boyle's Law illustrates pressure/volume relationships, and Charles's Law basically describes the effect of temperature changes on pressure and/or volume. The General Gas Law is a combination of these two laws. It is used to predict the behavior of a given quantity of gas when changes may be expected in any or all of the variables. The formula for the General Gas Law is:

$$\frac{P_1 V_1}{T_1} = \frac{P_2 V_2}{T_2}$$

Where P_1 = initial pressure (absolute)
   V_1 = initial volume
   T_1 = initial temperature (absolute)
   P_2 = final pressure (absolute)
   V_2 = final volume
   T_2 = final temperature (absolute)

Dalton's Law: The total pressure exerted by a mixture of gases is equal to the sum of the pressures of each of the different gases making up the mixture—each gas setting as if it alone was present and occupied the total volume. The whole is equal to the sum of its parts and each part is not affected by any of the other parts. The pressure of any gas in the mixture is proportional to the number of molecules of that gas in the total volume. The pressure of each gas is called its partial pressure (pp), meaning its part of the whole. Dalton's Law is sometimes referred to as "the law of partial pressures." The formula for Dalton's Law is:

$$P_{Total} = PP_A + PP_B + PP_C \ldots \ldots$$

   and

$$PP_A = P_{Total} \times \frac{\%\ Vol\cdot_A}{100\%}$$

Where P_{Total} = Total absolute pressure of gas mixture
   PP_A = Partial pressure of gas A
   PP_B = Partial pressure of gas B
   PP_C = Partial pressure of gas C

Henry's Law: The amount of a gas that will dissolve in a liquid at a given temperature is almost directly proportional to the partial pressure of that gas. If one unit of gas dissolves in a liquid at one atmosphere, then two units will dissolve at two atmospheres, three units at three atmospheres, and so on.

Buoyancy Control, Wet Suits, and Weight Belts

On the surface with air in their vests, the divers are too buoyant to descend. So they must purge this air by pushing or pulling a hand-operated valve near the vest mouth-

On the surface, inflated BC's allow you to rest whenever you want.

piece. (The valve and mouthpiece are at the end of a rubber hose which attaches high on the vest where water pressure from below tends to position the trapped air.) To eliminate the air, the divers might float with feet extending straight down and the hose held high with its valve depressed. By doing this, the air is automatically forced down the hose due to water pressure rising up their bodies as they sink.

If the divers are properly weighted with weight belts they'll achieve neutral buoyancy and neither sink nor rise at a point where their eyes break just above the water's surface. Because their vests are now empty of air, they're no longer positively buoyant and can descend. They'll now switch from snorkel to scuba and can simply swim down to a desired depth. As they descend, they'll find another reason to be glad they're wearing BC's.

Probably, they are also wearing wet suits. Because of this, they will have to put more air in their vests at some point if they want to remain "weightless" or neutrally buoyant. This is because a wet suit contains trapped nitrogen bubbles in its closed-cell rubber material. At 33 feet, these bubbles have been compressed to a much smaller volume than they had been at the surface. No longer are they subjected to 14.7 pounds pressure per square inch as they were above the water, they now experience twice the pressure, or 29.4 psi. Such reduced volume in the wet suit naturally means less mass to displace water, thus less buoyancy, and the divers will tend to sink. Since it is tiring to swim horizontally while constantly fighting the gravitational pull downward, the divers solve this problem by adding some air to their vests. This added air offsets the buoyancy lost due to the wet suits being significantly compressed at 33 feet.

To inject air in their BC's underwater, the divers simply grasp their hose valves and mouthpieces in their left hands, and their regulators in their right. Each takes a breath off the regulator, holds the breath, removes the regulator, inserts the vest mouthpiece, presses the valve, and blows air into the vest. They may repeat this process several times until they've achieved neutral buoyancy at that depth. When they're finally satisfied that they're "weightless," they remove the vest mouthpieces and replace them with their regulators. Then they resume normal breathing.

If they should descend to a greater depth, they'd likely want to put more air in their vests because wet suit buoyancy would have again been reduced and they would once more be *negatively* buoyant.

Conversely, if they should rise to a lesser depth, they'd probably want to hold their BC hoses higher than their vests, depress the valve for a second, and thereby allow some air to be forced out by the surrounding water pressure.

If they did not purge air from their BC's as they ascended, the *reduced* water pressure up at the shallower

Harold Boehm shows how a BC is inflated through its mouthpiece.

depth would make the gas volume *expand* in both their wet suits and BC's, and they would have to continuously exert themselves to keep from rising too fast since they'd have then become too *positively* buoyant.

The key point to remember about buoyancy compensators is that they help you remain COMFORTABLE IN THE WATER. That ability to stay comfortable is really what safe sport diving is all about.

Balancing Your Buoyancy

Before divers began using BC's, they could still dive all right but there was a lot more for them to worry about in terms of being COMFORTABLE IN THE WATER. The reason is as follows:

When a diver wears a wet suit he must also wear a belt of lead weights to offset the buoyancy caused by millions of tiny nitrogen bubbles trapped in the wet suit material. Typically, he should consider three factors in determining how much weight to wear:

1. The buoyancy of the wet suit based on its size;
2. his body's natural tendency to sink or float— everyone has different buoyancy in water;
3. the depth at which he'll be diving.

When these factors are determined, he can select and wear the combination of weights which will provide him neutral buoyancy at any preselected depth.

The problem with this approach is that he must remain very close to his predetermined depth or he'll constantly be fighting against negative or positive buoyancy. If this theoretical diver who is not using a BC stays at his neutrally buoyant depth, he is okay. But if he is constantly diving up and over reefs, cliffs, and inclines as is usual, thus experiencing wide variations in positive/negative buoyancy, he would tire faster than would the diver of today who'd use his BC to maintain weightlessness no matter what the depth.

BC's and Safety

Avoiding getting tired—that is the beauty of the BC and the reason why tremendous endurance is less critical a factor today in scuba diving than it was even ten years ago. Back then, you had to be in absolute top shape to fight constantly against negative/positive buoyancy. Today, though you should still maintain especially good physical condition, you simply *compensate* for a sinking or rising condition by varying the amount of air contained in a bag strapped to your body. The exertion of an average dive is thereby greatly reduced plus you're not so limited to staying at one predetermined depth. In addition, there's the comfortable feeling of knowing your vest will easily support you at the water's surface any time you choose.

When a diver is at the surface without a BC, he has to tread water as he breathes through his snorkel. This is fine so long as the diver is not tired because, under controlled conditions, a good snorkel will supply a diver's lungs with plenty of air. As he becomes winded or tired, however, he will need many times his regular air volume. A snorkel simply can't deliver enough air.

Each year, a few divers not wearing BC's become exhausted at the surface then, while excited or scared, try to breathe through a snorkel which cannot possibly deliver the volume of air they need to recover. Since they do not have BC's to inflate at the surface and support them high enough so that they can breathe directly through their mouths, they must tread water to stay up or breathe inadequately through their snorkels. Unless help is handy, they could tire and drown. If they're wearing a buoyant wet suit and counterbalancing weight belt, they could always save themselves by simply unhooking and releasing this weight belt. Unfortunately, simple solutions are frequently overlooked in panic situations.

Remember, we have said that a wet suit is very buoyant and that its buoyancy must be offset by weight attached to

BC's are a boon to safe diving, they reduce fatigue.

the body. Well, if the diver in trouble at the surface simply eliminates that weight, his wet suit will provide him all the buoyancy he'd ever need to keep his head well above the water. He could rest and then make his way to safety. Obviously, wearing a wet suit and weight belt adds a certain measure of safety to diving.

This safety factor is usually not available to those who dive in warm waters requiring no wet suit for insulation against cold. In such warm water diving, it is particularly important always to wear a BC. This is because a diver lacking both a wet suit and a BC has absolutely no extra flotation tool available if he exhausts himself on the surface.

Without a BC, he has nothing to rely upon for buoyancy except his natural tendency to float. Unless he remembers to float on his back or has perfected some other "drown proof" technique such as taught in Fred Lanove's book *Drownproofing,* he's in trouble unless his buddy or someone else can help him.

A Dive Before the Days of BC's

In the early days, some divers who'd otherwise be with us today were lost because BC's weren't available then. Consider the diver about vintage 1964 who weighted himself for neutral buoyancy at 30 feet and intended to stay at about that depth. However, as he dives along at 30 feet with his buddy, he spots the gleam of an aluminum outboard motor boat which lies upside down on the edge of an underwater cliff about 65 feet down.

Through hand signals he convinces his buddy it's worth a close look since the motor seems to be still attached and everything looks pretty new. They both descend, and at 65 feet experience negative buoyancy due to wet suit compression. The resulting tendency to sink seems no big problem since they reach the boat some three feet from a cliff which drops off sharply. They counter negative buoyancy by moving along the bottom near the cliff in stand-up position, "walking" on their fin-tips up to the boat. Both of them mentally calculate that the water out from the cliff edge is very deep because the bottom is not at all visible.

On checking their tank air pressure gauges, each finds about 1,500 pounds of air left. They know from experience that 1,500 pounds at 60 feet should allow some 30 minutes before they run short of air and must surface. They see no real problem at this time.

The diver who first spotted the boat makes for the

motor. He waves happily at his buddy on discovering the motor is in "like new" condition. They know that by flooding the boat interior with air bubbles from their tanks, the boat can probably be floated to the surface. If they can do this, then perhaps they can gain a reward from the owner. Or, if he can't be found, they may just have found themselves a free boat.

Their hearts beat fast with the excitement as they lie flat on the rock at right angles to the inverted boat's bow and stern. Each man finds a break in the rocks large enough to stick his head beneath the boat, thus the otherwise wasted exhalation bubbles from the regulator exhausts can rise beneath the boat and help displace water there. Periodically, they also push the purge valves on their regulators to release great billows of air bubbles which also become trapped at the highest point inside the overturned boat. Purging air from their tanks without first breathing it will displace water under the boat at a much greater rate than will the exhaust bubbles alone.

After a while, they are able to move the boat a few inches by hand but it is still far too heavy to rise by itself. Nonetheless, they realize that if they can kick hard with their fins and raise the boat from about 65 feet to 33 feet, the air trapped inside will have increased significantly in volume so that the boat should rise to the surface without further heavy kicking effort on their part.

They omit, however, to check their underwater tank pressure gauges once again, this would have told them air supplies were very low. They forget this because only a few minutes have elapsed since they started their task. Yet a great deal of air has already left their tanks both because of their increased breathing needs due to exertion and because they quickly used up a lot of air by purging it directly from their breathing supply into the boat cavity. They continue breathing with their heads under the gunwales. The boat suddenly shudders and moves a bit by itself.

They move to opposite sides of it, standing on the rock ledge with their fins flat on the rock. They grasp the gunwales and lift upwards. The boat is still heavy. They breathe very hard now. The boat rises slightly and moves laterally towards the cliff edge a bit. They lift harder. The first diver removes his regulator from his mouth and sticks it under the gunwale. He immediately pushes the regulator purge valve and releases a long blast of air bubbles. The second diver does the same. Both are now very tired but quite excited because the boat is rising more and more. They put their regulators back in their mouths and kick hard off the bottom. The boat moves with them, upwards and laterally out over the drop-off and the darkness below.

The two divers keep their bodies vertical, heads bent under the boat so their exhaust bubbles will continue displacing water. The boat rises upwards at a faster rate, though it seems to them to move very slowly. The two men have been diving together for years and they believe this boat to be their greatest prize.

But now the diver who first spotted the boat suddenly finds it a little hard to breathe. Both are still kicking very hard to keep the boat balanced and headed upwards. The first diver realizes the hardness of breathing means he is running low on air. This signal tells him he has only a few minutes of air left to breathe.

He reaches back to pull his tank reserve lever which would give him perhaps two or three more precious minutes of air, but he finds the reserve has somehow already been tripped. Probably while he was poking his head under the boat.

Now it is getting very hard for him to breathe. His legs are extremely tired from the prolonged hard kicking. It dawns on him he is still about 50 feet from the surface which is about a minute's swim at normal ascent rates. He holds on to the edge of the boat and continues kicking upwards. He moves faster now, still holding onto the boat, but he must suck very hard to get air.

In the back of his head a reflex spills onto his conscious thought and simply says to him, "Listen. No boat is worth dying for." With that he releases his side of the boat. As he does so, the boat's keel turns toward him because his buddy continues pushing upward on the opposite side. The boat rolls and pitches quickly towards him, belching a mountain of air bubbles. They expand above him in their flight to the surface.

He now takes long, sucking breaths on his regulator. It is exactly the limited-air feeling one gets when breathing through a soda pop straw. The boat settles in a billow of sediment back down on the rock.

Since he is weighted for 30 feet he is negatively buoyant at 50 feet. Thus, he sinks down past the boat and in a few seconds he can no longer see the boat above him atop the cliff. As he looks up he sees his buddy some 60 feet higher.

Now he's alone. And he knows he must fight to keep his calm and think hard or he'll continue sinking to the bottom with virtually no air. He knows that doing so means certain death.

The diver struggles to relax his mind and body, overcoming the panic he knows he'll be unable to control in another 30 seconds. The solution is simple. He's used it before.

He unhitches his weight belt and drops it to one side so it does not catch on his knife or fin. Immediately he stops sinking. At 75 feet down without the weight belt, the wet suit gives him a few pounds of positive buoyance. He rises very slowly. He is not swimming. His legs seem dead.

The diver knows from experience that as he rises, the volume of nitrogen trapped in his wet suit material will expand, causing him to rise even faster. He also knows that the little volume of the air remaining in his diving tank will go further as he rises upwards into reduced ambient pressure so he can soon breathe easier if he can only hold out a few seconds more. He feels the dizziness caused by his prolonged sucking for the trickle of air from the regulator. He must rise even faster to expand that air volume. His mind is filled with the thought that somehow he must *breathe* again!

He flutters his fin tips with his dangling legs which feel slightly better now. He uses them mechanically, in a slow, stiff-kneed kick. With this, his upward speed seems suddenly to double. He looks downward at the boat as he passes it by, rising above the cliff's edge. He kicks a bit harder, trying to stay calm, concentrating on working his weakened legs in an efficient kick. He carefully adds to each kick a stronger flip of the fin tips. This will bring more speed with minimal effort.

Having risen upwards a ways, the air he breathed into his lungs at 75 feet has expanded and he feels less of a need now to breathe. He glances below and guesses he is at about a 50 foot depth. He forces himself upwards even faster. As he goes, he exhales a bit then sucks on the regulator and finds the breathing is a little easier now. He takes in the thin amount of air slowly, in a long, even breath. He exhales it slowly. He remembers not to hold his breath as he passes upward alongside a kelp stalk and through a cloud of two-inch-long grey fish with extremely large spiny dorsal fins.

He knows that if he did rise while holding his breath, his lungs would expand virtually to the bursting point or beyond. And that this would kill or cripple him upon reaching the surface which he sees is now only about 30 feet above. He sees the light, there, shining off the waves, and his legs feel stronger. The compressed air from his tank is expanding. He regularly breathes it in and out as he rises.

At a depth of 30 feet the wet suit has greatly expanded

from its point of highest compression when he was at 75 feet. He breathes a bit more easily now from the regulator because the compressed air from his tank can expand more in the shallower water.

The wet suit becomes increasingly buoyant, causing him to rise even faster. But he knows that so long as he exhales almost continuously his lungs will probably not have a chance to become overinflated, thereby causing a dangerous embolism. He knows now that with air in his lungs he will be all right.

From 30 feet on, the diver does not swim upwards at all. He knows his body has been under high pressure at 75 feet and now he is rising far too quickly toward the low pressure surface. He has made the ascent from 75 feet in much, much less than a minute. Rising that fast presents another problem which, as an experienced diver, he deals with immediately.

He knows that just as the air in his lungs expanded rapidly as he rose upwards into water of *lesser* pressure, so did the nitrogen which was forced into solution in his blood stream by *higher* pressure when he was down at 75 feet. He knows he must not take a chance on getting "the bends" (a function of nitrogen coming out of solution and forming bubbles inside blood and tissue).

To slow this too rapid ascent he's making into a reduced pressure region, he flares out his body in spread-eagle fashion to increase drag even as he *continues rising* up to the 20 foot level. His buoyant wet suit keeps him rising, but flaring-out slows this rate considerably. He breathes very little, exhaling most of the time to prevent lung over-expansion. He feels relieved that his mind is working fine. Otherwise, he'd never have thought about the bends or about embolism.

He remembers learning in his training that nitrogen in the air he breathes goes into solution in his blood when under the pressure of depth. The only way a body can get rid of this dissolved gas is through normal respiration. He remembers the instructor pointing out that if his body contains dissolved nitrogen at a pressure exceeding twice the pressure around him, bubbles will form in his blood stream and tissues. If allowed to develop, these bubbles would block circulation, destroy tissue, or maybe even lodge in the brain, nerves, or spinal cord. By staying under pressure longer, by prolonging his breathing a while more before he reaches the surface with its relatively low pressure, the diver knows his body should have enough time to give off this nitrogen as a gas instead of have it form dangerous bubbles inside his system. He remembers that his scuba instructor compared the bends to the way bubbles come out of solution when a soda bottle is uncapped. Fortunately, the diver is familiar with specific U.S. Navy tables which cover decompression times at various depths, as well as recommended rates of ascent under varying conditions.

The rising diver is flared-out and facing upward. He looks upwards to ensure he is not under the boat or any other obstacle. Now he is thinking clearly and is proud of the way he has behaved under stress.

Suddenly he breaks through the water's surface. He rights himself, very buoyant in his full wet suit without the weight belt. He rolls onto his back and breathes in great volumes of fresh air again. He relaxes himself totally, looking up at the clouds in the blue sky. He floats there, arms and legs dangling loosely as his wet suit's flotation easily supports him.

A voice calls his name from behind and his buddy fins up around in front of him. His buddy is surprised because when they parted company at 75 feet, our diver was hopelessly sinking downward.

"You okay for sure?" the buddy asks as his eyes probe for symptoms of the bends or signs of various other diving maladies. Our diver smiles and nods that he is all right.

The buddy says, "You rest awhile, then we'll go to the boat. It's just over there."

The diver curls a fin to turn, and looks around behind him. The boat is about 50 yards away. The crew members and some divers on deck are all watching them. One crew member is holding a flotation doughnut with a rope attached. The buddy gives an "OK" sign with one hand and hollers to them, "He's okay. We'll swim it in a few minutes."

For awhile the two divers lie on the water. Then side by side, they snorkel slowly back to the boat. The buddy reaches over and grabs our diver's shoulder. They stop and look at each other.

The buddy removes his snorkel and says, "There wasn't anything I could do down there. I had to leave you. You understand?"

Our diver spits out his snorkel, puts his hands on both the buddy's shoulders and says to him, "Hey, I understand. You'd have been crazy to come after me. Forget that part of it because it's over and I'm okay. I'd have had to do the same thing with you and you know it." They smile at each other a moment and go on to the waiting boat.

The Buoyancy Compensator   25

All around them it is a very fine day for diving. Our diver was lucky. He was also able to stay incredibly calm. He was experienced enough to survive. Nine out of ten divers wouldn't have survived in his situation without a BC.

Now let's see what difference a BC would make in the same diving experience.

The Same Dive Today, with BC's

The same two divers enter the water wearing BC's. Again, each man wears a full wet suit and enough weights to provide neutral buoyancy at 30 feet. (Ideally, they would weight themselves for neutral buoyancy at the surface.) At almost 30 feet down, the first diver spots the boat and descends toward it with his buddy. At about 45 feet, they stop a moment and both experience the sinking feeling of being negatively buoyant. They both blow air into their vests then hover at 45 feet testing themselves for neutral buoyancy. Satisfied, they head on down to the boat which is near the edge of the underwater cliff.

Again, they are excited because of the new condition of the boat but not so excited that they forget about buoyancy control. Even though they had stopped at 45 feet and blown air into their vests, this air has continued to *decrease* in volume as they approached the sunken boat resting at 65 feet. Also decreased was the volume of nitrogen bubbles trapped in their wet suits. As a result, upon reaching 65 feet, they were once again negatively buoyant. This is immediately apparent to them because they cannot hover. Instead they must push upwards off the bottom now and then with their fins.

Both men are wearing medium-large volume BC's, capable of about 40 pounds positive buoyancy when *fully* inflated. Before touching the boat, they blow into their vests just enough air to achieve neutral buoyancy. They know when this point is reached because at neutral buoyancy they will rise very slightly when they inhale and sink very slightly when they exhale. The average of this respiration process provides them with neutral buoyancy.

The divers gesture back and forth with hand signals as to how they will try raising the boat by filling its cavity with air bubbles which will float it to the surface.

They poke their heads under the gunwales and breathe so that their regulators' exhaust bubbles are trapped under the boat. After they do this, a quick check of their pressure gauges shows 1,500 pounds of air remaining in their tanks or approximately 30 minutes of air at 60 feet.

They purge large volumes of air directly from their regulators into the overturned boat's hull. After a while, the boat moves upwards a few inches and sideways towards the drop-off. The divers notice this sidewards movement and realize that because the heavy motor is toward the drop-off, the boat will naturally move out over the cliff at some point during the ascent.

The first diver taps on the boat hull and stands up. His buddy, hearing the knocking, does the same. They look at each other over the boat. The first diver holds up his BC hose and mouthpiece and points at it. The buddy nods, and points an index finger at his head as though to say, "You're thinking."

They both lie back down on the rock and breathe up inside the boat. It moves much easier now. They find that by standing flat on their fins and lifting, they can raise it a few inches. They decide to borrow a bit of buoyancy from their BC's as an aid to lifting the boat. Knowing that it is a dangerous procedure to fill a BC then distribute that lifting force to some other object through your body, the divers only partially, not *fully,* inflate their vests. However, the safest way to lift the boat would be through use of a "lift bag" especially designed for such purposes.

They take deep breaths on their regulators, then remove them from their mouths. They blow about two thirds of the breath into their BC mouthpieces, then breathe again from their regulators. This process is repeated several times. The increased buoyancy causes them to rise so they must hold onto the boat gunwales or otherwise float upwards. Because both men have partially inflated vests, contribution of buoyancy toward raising the boat is some 30 pounds or the equivalent air volume of about three basketballs at the surface.

Actually, the boat, since it is underwater, weighs much less than it would at the surface. This is because Archimedes' Law states that "an object immersed in a liquid will be buoyed upward by a force equal to the weight of the liquid it displaces." Since this boat is totally underwater, it is displacing a significant amount of water which weighs 64 pounds per cubic foot—the figure is for salt water; fresh water weighs 62.4 pounds per cubic foot. The boat is "lighter" underwater in direct proportion to the amount of the displaced water.

Because this law of physics always applies underwater, and because of the additional 30 pounds of buoyancy gained from the two divers partially filling their vests, the boat starts slowly upwards.

As it rises, it swings out over the cliff. At this point neither diver is tired from excessive lifting or kicking, since they have let their BC's help them do part of the work.

The hands of the first diver, however, accidentally slips off the gunwale and the boat overturns, spilling its air and sinking at an angle back down onto the cliff. Both divers *immediately* hold up their BC hoses and vent their vests. They rise a few feet before they can release enough air to provide neutral buoyancy once again. Had they not vented air immediately, they could have quickly risen to lower pressures where the BC air might be expanding faster than it could be dumped. This could prove even more dangerous than the too rapid ascent of the pre-BC diver in the earlier example of the same dive. But our divers, skilled with BC's, recognized the potential danger before it even was upon them. (Some large-volume BC's feature an "emergency dump valve" which allows particularly rapid discharge of air. This feature is of much value in helping a diver prevent an uncontrolled, too rapid ascent.)

The divers join each other and hover together above the deep area below, shrugging and smiling—as much as one can when puckered like a carp around a regulator mouthpiece. They gesture to forget the boat.

They do not swim or use their feet at all as they rise. They ascend extremely slowly up to 50 feet then begin rising faster. Recalling their training in scuba diving, they realize they should not rise faster than 60 feet a minute in order to avoid the bends. For simplicity in determining this ideal rate of ascent, they watch their smallest exhaust bubbles rise. They've learned that if they rise at the speed of the smallest exhaust bubbles, they'll be ascending at approximately 60 feet per minute. And this amount of time spent in rising will safely allow the nitrogen, which is in solution in their blood, to vent itself naturally out through their lungs as a gas. Rising at a faster rate might cause the nitrogen to come out of solution as bubbles in their blood stream. So to slow down, the divers vent air from their vests.

To do this, they hold their BC hoses above the highest point of their vests. In this way, water pressure will force the air upwards and toward the valve at the end of the hoses. When they depress the one-way valve, the air is free, blasting upwards from the hose mouthpiece.

The divers continue this venting until their vests are nearly flat against them. Venting the air slows their ascent to about 40 feet per minute. They know this because they see that the smaller exhaust bubbles are now rising faster than they are.

When they reach the 33-foot depth, their vests begin expanding rapidly in size due to the greatly reduced exterior pressure. In fact, between 33 feet and the surface, the air volume of their BC's will actually double since the water pressure is reduced by 50 percent in that final distance. Because of this, the divers continue venting air all the way to the top.

As they rise, they look upwards and hold their hoses up with an arm extended to guard against running into objects. They have breathed regularly in and out all the way up from the depths in order to avoid overexpanding their lungs as they rose.

At the surface, both divers still have their weight belts on and are relaxed and feel strong. They orally inflate their vests a bit more, rest a moment talking about the "motor boat that got away," and then snorkel back to the charter dive boat.

Each diver still has about 300 pounds of air, or 3-5 minutes of breathing time, in his tank. This is good, since one should ideally hit the surface with about this amount remaining. Having a few hundred pounds of air after a dive helps prevent interior tank corrosion during storage periods, plus it could be useful should our divers surface and find a kelp bed or other surface obstruction between them and the boat. The divers have been taught a technique for swimming on the surface over kelp, but it is far easier to use scuba and simply pass below obstacles.

It's apparent which of the two dives just described was the easiest, safest, and most fun. Why was it the latter dive? Because of the BC's the divers wore, and because of the training they'd received in the use of this wonderfully simple device.

The point cannot be too strongly stressed: TO BE COMFORTABLE IN THE WATER, DIVE WITH A BUOYANCY COMPENSATOR.

4
Is Scuba Diving Expensive?

Care in Selection

There is a mistaken belief that scuba diving is very expensive. However, this is only another myth. For about the same price as a complete set of good golf clubs and accessories, one can buy all the basic equipment needed for scuba. This cost will be from $400-$700 if you buy all new gear.

If, for economic reasons, you must buy used scuba gear, be absolutely certain that a qualified equipment specialist thoroughly examines each item before you buy it. Remember, diving is about 60 percent brains, and part of being smart about diving is making sure your gear is always capable of top performance.

Just because a piece of gear seems to do what it's supposed to do when you check it at the surface does not mean it will continue working that way at 33 feet down, where the pressure on all its moving parts has *doubled*. In addition, you as a novice diver are certainly no competent judge of even minimum standards of equipment performance. For example, maybe you "test" that used regulator you bought and find that it easily delivers air when it's connected to a dive tank. So what does that prove? You are at this point very unaware of regulator performance characteristics.

Do you know how to hold a regulator to your ear and listen for freeflow sounds which means air will be used up at a far faster rate than normal at depth? Can you sit in your living room and determine how easily the regulator will exhaust your breaths at a 50-foot depth? Well, then, exercise your mind before you dive and have all used gear checked by a specialist if you truly feel you must buy used gear. Remember, that piece of used gear may have been sitting in someone's dirty garage for the last two years before its exterior was cleaned up for sale to you.

If that's the case, the interior could be filled with rust or galvanic corrosion from the attack of salt water. In addition, rubber parts may be weakened or rotted from ozone or simply old age. In other words, the used gear may perform as perfectly as a brand new item, but it could also cease functioning tomorrow, though, typically, good diving gear is quite "bug free." The solution? Use brain power. Have any used gear carefully checked, particularly gear bought from a private party. This will cost you a few dollars but, then, so does a polio shot.

Cost of New Equipment

Let us assume you buy all new gear. Even if you do this, you should still have each item carefully examined for proper *function* by the equipment specialist at the dive store where the piece was purchased. After all, dive stores have hundreds of boxes of diving equipment and there is a very small chance you might have an extremely rare manufactured "lemon." Better find out for sure. Why take chances?

One final point on "lemons." Major diving equipment manufacturers all have rigid quality control standards for inspecting the equipment they make. Therefore, there is only a small possibility that a newly manufactured piece of gear will malfunction. Nonetheless, have it looked at anyway for your own safety and peace of mind.

If you do enough careful shopping and look for sales, your new scuba gear may cost as little as $375. However, no matter how much you spend, this cost should be viewed as being amortized over a good many years of use. Good scuba gear lasts a long time if it's properly maintained. Some firms even offer lifetime warranties on tanks and regulators. So over ten years' use the initial cost comes down to only a few dollars annually, if we don't count miscellaneous small repairs, strap replacements, and perhaps one new mask or so during this period.

Here are some price ranges for the most frequently used pieces of scuba gear. Remember, however, that during your basic scuba certification course, all gear that is considered scuba per se is often provided by the instructor. Normally, because of the need for a proper fit, instructors will require that you purchase your own mask, snorkel, and fins. Occasionally, usage of a wet suit (if required for insulation against cold) is included as part of the course cost. In addition, many dive stores offering instruction today allow you use of a buoyancy compensator as part of the package. There is, however, no universal rule on what pieces of gear you'll find included in the cost of your course.

Underwater Compass

Because your basic scuba instruction course will first teach you how to snorkel dive before exposing you to use of any scuba gear, it's very important that your snorkeling gear is of high quality. This means that the mask and fins fit properly and that the snorkel is comfortable, as well as allowing easy breathing. (Selection of the right mask, snorkel, and fins is covered in Chapter 5.) Typically, however, the best fitting, best performing gear will be in the mid to top price range. Examine *good* beginning gear in these price ranges:

SKIN DIVING EQUIPMENT

	$	$
Mask	9 to	25
Snorkel	4 to	8
Fins	14 to	28
Boots	8 to	16
Buoyancy Compensator* with CO_2 cartridge	35 to	150

Total: $70–$227

*Sometimes optional, depending on the instructor, during the snorkel diving part of a scuba course.

Underwater depth gauge

71.2 cubic ft. steel air cylinder with K-valve

Single hose, two-stage regulator

	$	$
71.2 cubic ft. steel air cylinder with valve	50 to	125
(or)		
Aluminum air cylinder* with valve	(150 to	225)
Single hose, two stage regulator	75 to	160
Single cylinder backpack	20 to	40
Noncustom, 2-piece wet suit, 1/4" thickness	50 to	140
Underwater tank pressure gauge	25 to	80
Weight belt	5 to	7
20 pounds of lead weights	25 to	40
Accessories		
Diving knife	15 to	45
Underwater depth gauge	10 to	55
Gear Bag	1 to	30
Underwater compass	10 to	30
Underwater diving watch	75 to	200
	361 to	1052

Total: $431 to $1279

*Aluminum tank price not included in total.

Single cylinder back-pack

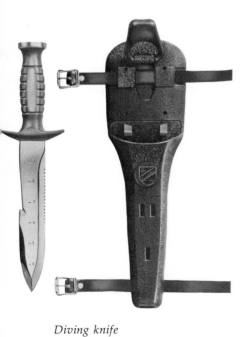

Diving knife

Underwater diving watch

A good mask, snorkel, and fins to start scuba diving can cost less than $30. Add $50 to $75 for the certification course itself (which frequently includes some rental of scuba gear) and you can become a certified scuba diver for around $100.

Often, the more expensive pieces of scuba equipment can be bought when "on sale," or during off-season months when demand for gear is lower. Large dive stores sometimes accept payment on a credit basis over a period of six months or a year. If a time-payment plan suits your needs, use the Yellow Pages to locate those dive shops offering such service. Ideally, though, *never* purchase equipment other than mask, snorkel, and fins until you've successfully *completed* a scuba diving course. The reason is simply that, if for some reason you don't finish the course, the gear will be of no use to you except, perhaps, at a garage sale.

Recurring Costs

There are recurring costs associated with scuba diving. Each time you refill your dive tanks, the dive store or boat will charge you between $1.00 and $2.50 for this service. In addition, you'll regularly use certain special powders, lubricants, and preservatives on your equipment. These costs, however, are relatively minor.

Should you not have free access to a boat, you'll find that scuba charter boats charge each diver-passenger from $15 to $30 for a day's diving. If you belong to a diving club or arrange for your boat dives through a local dive store, sometimes a "group" rate—which is usually much lower than the individual rate—is available. If you plan on doing all of your diving from a beach, naturally you'll not be worrying about charter boat costs.

Cost of Underwater Photography Gear

After you've been diving a while, you may want to invest in special equipment for underwater photography. Good underwater photo gear is usually quite expensive since it must be built to withstand extreme variations of pressure, yet remain airtight and watertight.

Before you get into mixing cameras and diving, however, you'd be wise to buy from your dive store or borrow from the library a book on basic underwater photography. This will tell you precisely how best to get started. You'd be smart also to have your instructor or dive store owner put you in touch with a local amateur underwater photographer or club. Remember, before investing in underwater photo equipment, be sure to read one or two of the many books on the subject, and talk with people who are already skilled in the hobby.

After making your study, you may want to start by purchasing a waterproof housing for your instamatic-type or 35mm camera. If the dive shop doesn't have this enclosure in stock, they can show you catalogs from which to order a watertight housing to fit your camera. These vary in price. An enclosure for the cheapest instamatic-type camera starts at about $30.

Finally, if your budget can stand it, you might look at the several 35mm cameras especially designed for underwater use. The most popular model is the Nikonos II made by Nikon. By the time you buy such a camera, you can have invested about $300. Yet, properly cared for, the outfit should last you a lifetime.

Cost of Spearfishing Equipment

Gear for spearfishing is not very expensive. You can buy a very good Hawaiian sling or pole spear for under $20. However, it would be a good idea to take a special course—if one is available in spearfishing techniques—from an instructor before trying this sport. At the very least, you should thoroughly discuss it with your diving instructor or dive store owner before you even buy a spear, let alone use one. Remember, spears and spearguns are weapons for killing. And without thorough knowledge of their proper use, you could seriously injure yourself or someone else. However, once you become experienced at spearfishing, it's a safe, fun-filled activity. In addition, it's a great way to bring gourmet seafood to the table at a price far below supermarket costs.

Scuba Accessories

You can easily spend thousands of dollars on all kinds of scuba-related accessories. Some items you might consider first include: a rubber tank boot, "goodie" bag for collecting shells, lobsters, and etc., a drawstring instrument bag, underwater light, hood, gloves, boots, decompression meter, thermometer, cushioned case for protecting gauges and fragile items, plus a very large gear bag for carrying and keeping all your basic scuba equipment in one place—except, of course, your tank.

This kind of accessory equipment is especially handy to have, but by no means essential for a beginning diver.

The one exception to this statement would be the gear bag. Equipment gets marred or damaged when beginning divers carry equipment loose in their arms or rolling around the trunk of a car. A suitable gear bag helps prevent damage to equipment. It also helps ensure that your personal items are less likely to be accidentally mixed in with another diver's gear. Gear bags can either be those specially designed for scuba divers or a heavy gauge army surplus bag, which does the job very nicely at a fairly low purchase price.

5 Choosing Scuba Equipment

Mask

You wear a mask when diving to give you unblurred underwater vision and to protect your eyes and nose from impurities in the water. When open underwater, the human eye distorts vision in much the same way as it would if the eyeball had extreme astigmatism.

Without a mask, things underwater become blurs and shadows, but with a mask, vision is normal except for one major difference—objects underwater appear 25 percent larger and closer. Thus, a three-foot fish may look four feet long and a fish four feet away looks three feet away.

After your first few dives, however, you'll find yourself compensating for this distortion and you'll learn to reach for objects where they really are and not where they appear to be.

The best mask for the *beginner* fits your face comfortably and doesn't leak underwater. In addition, it is of "low volume" which means it traps very little air between the

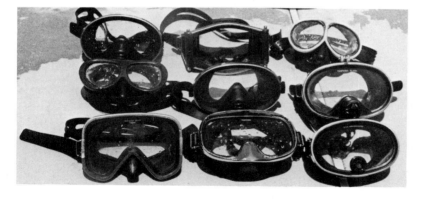

Don't be confused by the wide choice of masks facing you. As a beginner, stick with smaller, low-volume masks for maximum comfort and overall ease of use.

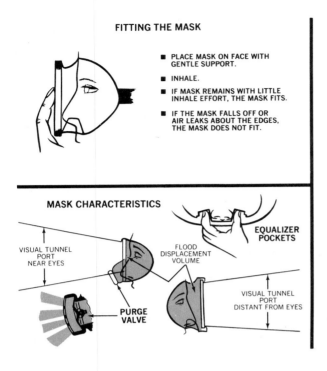

FITTING THE MASK

- PLACE MASK ON FACE WITH GENTLE SUPPORT.
- INHALE.
- IF MASK REMAINS WITH LITTLE INHALE EFFORT, THE MASK FITS.
- IF THE MASK FALLS OFF OR AIR LEAKS ABOUT THE EDGES, THE MASK DOES NOT FIT.

MASK CHARACTERISTICS

VISUAL TUNNEL PORT NEAR EYES

FLOOD DISPLACEMENT VOLUME

EQUALIZER POCKETS

PURGE VALVE

VISUAL TUNNEL PORT DISTANT FROM EYES

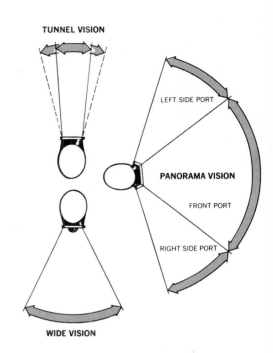

TUNNEL VISION

LEFT SIDE PORT

PANORAMA VISION

FRONT PORT

RIGHT SIDE PORT

WIDE VISION

lens and your face. This is important because sooner or later any mask you choose will be disturbed during a dive and will allow water to interfere with your vision. When this happens, you'll want to "clear" it quickly by exhaling through your nose and displacing the water with air. The smaller the mask's volume, the simpler becomes this task.

Bigger volume masks are used most frequently by divers using scuba. This is because they have plenty of air in a tank for clearing water from a mask. However, smaller volume masks also provide good peripheral vision, so this is another reason they're preferred by more and more snorkel and scuba divers today.

Pat Anderson tests a low-volume mask for fit. Because of his moustache, Anderson rubs petroleum jelly below his nose before a dive to help create an airtight seal.

Judy Leite presses a mask against her face and inhales through her nose.

The mask stays sealed in place, thus it probably will not leak during underwater use.

FITTING A MASK

In a dive store you'll see dozens of mask styles on display. As a beginning diver, test five or six of the smaller masks (not goggles) for fit. Here's how this is done: Move the head strap out of the way atop the mask and spread the rubber feather-edges apart. Place the mask carefully over your eyes and nose, ensuring the feather-edges aren't bent under, and hold the mask against your face until it seems to feel best. Then inhale gently through your nose. Block off this inhalation while it's in progress by swallowing and holding the swallow about halfway through.

By inhaling gently then stopping, you have created a partial vacuum inside the mask. The vacuum should draw the mask tighter against the face. If it doesn't, because of air seeping in between the face and the mask edges, rearrange the mask slightly on your face and try this process several more times. Be sure no strands of hair are caught in the seal because this will surely cause leakage. Sometimes puckering your lips under the mask will make it seal better under your nose. This is also the position your lips will be in most of the time, since while diving a snorkel or regulator will usually be in your mouth.

Repeat the test for proper seal on all the masks you've selected. Then, through the process of elimination discover which one feels most comfortable while also sealing the best.

Once you've made your choice, adjust the split head

Be sure the mask you choose has a "tempered glass" marking on the lens or is otherwise shatter resistant for safety.

strap to fit snugly, but not tightly, just above and below that bump on the back of your head. Wear the mask around the store for a few minutes. If the mask still seems comfortable and seals tightly, you may want to buy it. But first ask a few questions.

EVALUATING MASK FEATURES

Ask the salesperson if your mask selection is a suitable piece of *professional quality* scuba diving equipment. If it is, then it likely has a double-edge seal construction and a tempered glass lens which is shatter resistant.

Don't ever buy a mask with a plastic lens. Plastic lenses fog badly underwater and scratch easily.

Also, never buy, or even use a mask, which has a snorkel tube (or tubes) supplying air directly into the mask. Those little snorkel devices featuring a Ping-Pong ball inside a cage often leak very badly. They are unsafe toys. Never use them in skin or scuba diving.

Choose a mask with a firmly locking but adjustable separate head strap, preferably one with a split band in the back for extra comfort. The mask you choose *does not* fit over the mouth; only over your nose and eyes.

As a final check of your mask selection, after purchase, show it to a diver friend or your scuba instructor. All they have to tell you is whether or not it's a good scuba mask. It's unimportant whether they'd buy the same brand or style. Only that, in their opinion, it's a good scuba mask made by a reputable manufacturer. Be sure to save your sales receipt until you're sure the mask that was both comfortable and fit well was truly a scuba-quality mask. People who normally wear glasses can have prescription-ground lenses attached inside their masks.

A snorkel lets you breathe while your face is underwater.

Snorkel

A snorkel is worn so that you can breathe without the effort of raising some of your body weight out of the water each time you need air. A snorkel also lets you cruise along the surface without taking your eyes off events and objects passing below you. And finally, it helps you conserve your air supply before and after using scuba.

You'll find less than a dozen basic snorkel designs in a dive store. Most snorkels are in a "J" or "L" shape. Some have a bellows-type flexible curve which lets the mouthpiece hang out of the way when a scuba regulator is being used. Thus, this type snorkel is convenient for alternating frequently between snorkel and a scuba regulator, plus its ability to flex means extra comfort for denture wearers. It's also less likely to snag on kelp or weeds; when this happens, it can pull off your mask. Such snorkels, however, occasionally trap a small amount of water in the accordion-like bellows—just enough so you're always "misting." This could become annoying, especially on a long snorkel swim. And such an annoyance is not conducive to BEING COMFORTABLE IN THE WATER. The key feature to look for in a snorkel is breathing ease and a tendency for it *not* to trap or collect water.

CHOOSING YOUR FIRST SNORKEL

As a beginner, you'll likely find the standard, large-bore, no nonsense J or L-shaped snorkel easiest to use. When shopping at the dive store, pick five or six J or L snorkels of medium bore diameter and ask a clerk to wash off each mouthpiece. When he returns, stick each snorkel in your mouth and see how the various ones conform to your jaw structure, teeth, and lips. Your choice should be approximately 12 to 15 inches long for easiest breathing.

SNORKELS AND COMFORT

Once again, you're looking above all for comfort. Because you're a neophyte, about all you can test for is "does it feel right?" You should particularly test to see if the flat flange which fits between your lips and gums tends to "cut" you, or if the nubs you hold in your teeth seem to be logistically mismatched to your dental equipment.

Don't feel confused if *all* the snorkels you try seem equally uncomfortable. Keep making comparisons and finally through process of elimination, make a choice. Later, at home, you might want to hook the snorkel to the *left* side of your mask (so the snorkel is near your left ear) and see how a snorkel feels in the mouth of a beginning diver after half an hour or so. You'll find your jaws have gotten dead tired, but that doesn't mean you picked the wrong snorkel. It just means your jaw muscles aren't yet ready to accept such a foreign piece for such a prolonged period. Go look in the mirror at your face. As you crack

Kathy Cully shows how a snorkel is held in the mouth.

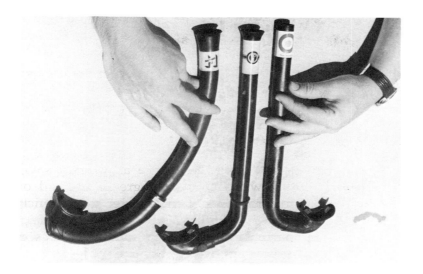

Snorkels come in varying shapes. A recent innovation is the flared-end tube which tests indicate can help improve breathing ease by about 18%.

up, you'll see why. (A snorkel is hooked to the left side because a single hose regulator is designed to come over the right shoulder. In this way, the two breathing devices keep out of each other's way.)

Much later, after your fifth or sixth hour of snorkel diving, if you still have a sore mouth or gums, see about getting a snorkel with a *smaller* or differently shaped mouthpiece. Some manufacturers now offer a mouthpiece which conforms exactly to the bite-print of your teeth for an extremely comfortable fit. You might ask your instructor and other divers for their opinion on this innovation. It seems to satisfy those currently using it.

The snorkel on the left has a bellows-flex curve so it falls well out of the way when a diver switches to a scuba regulator.

Choosing Scuba Equipment   43

Another recent improvement to snorkels is a funnel-shaped, belled flange at the intake end of the snorkel tube. This flange tends to direct incoming and outgoing air properly and make it less turbulent. Bench tests of air flow rates indicate that, in a diver's normal breathing range, the amount of air moved for a given breathing effort is increased significantly by the funnel shape. During 1976, several major manufacturers were offering in their line at least one snorkel with this advantage.

Some snorkels are available now with a mouthpiece which rotates 30 degrees at the end of the tube. This rotation makes it much easier to quickly and correctly position the snorkel. You might find this feature to be of particular advantage in your early days of pool and open-water diving experience.

One can even buy a snorkel featuring a purge valve at the bottom part of the J below the mouthpiece. It seems there is little value in having a purge valve on a snorkel, since purging of water is done by you simply blowing up into the tube. Also, a purge valve is just another equipment modification which *could* go wrong.

Fins

Fins are worn to propel you through the water with more power and with far greater ease than would bare feet. In water, your leg muscles are strong enough to push feet many times the size of yours.

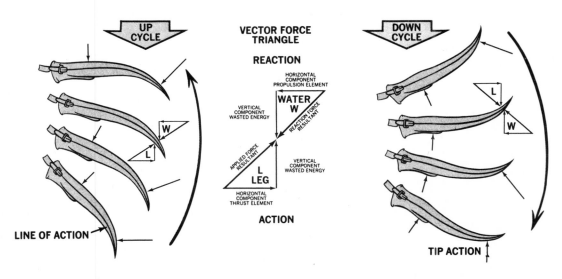

Fin propulsion is a practical application of Newton's third law of motion: "Every action is opposed by an equal and opposite reaction." Leg and ankle muscles versus water resistance.

The fin types displayed by Kathy Cully and Harold Boehm are (L-R): (1) full foot, (2) open heel, nonadjustable (UDT-type), (3) open-heel, strap adjustable, vented, and (4) open-heel, strap adjustable, nonvented.

No matter what type, fins should always be comfortable and of the right size for your leg muscles. Barb Steiner (left) prefers smaller full-foot fins, while Kathy Cully chooses larger open-heeled ones.

Fins which are too flexible waste your energy. Fins which are too large or stiff bring on cramps because they tire your leg muscles.

In a dive store you'll see almost as many types and sizes of fins as you will masks. But all you really care about is fit. Select fins exactly as you would a pair of good shoes, except that with fins you should completely ignore how they look. If the fins have open heels, you should try them on while wearing Neoprene diving boots which are a great comfort feature combined with this type of fin.

Usually, colored buoyant fins are more flexible than standard black ones.

TYPES OF FINS

Typically, fins fall into two categories: full foot and open heel. No matter what type you select, they should be snug but not cut off circulation.

Fins which are too tight will cause cramps and minimize the amount of blood reaching your feet. If fins are too loose, you'll probably get blisters, and certainly chafing.

As a beginner, consider sticking for a while with the more flexible fins until your leg muscles are used to the extra effort. Colored floating fins are usually more flexible than black rubber sinking ones.

NEOPRENE BOOTS WITH FINS

If you'll be diving in colder waters where a wet suit is required, you'll probably be wearing neoprene boots inside an open-heeled fin. Such fins are far easier to get on

Neoprene diving boots.

Choosing Scuba Equipment   45

and off over boots than are full-foot fins. This is due to the rubber-to-rubber friction problems of cramming a compressible boot inside a foot pocket. Only about half the boot is inserted into a strap-adjustable fin and doing this is relatively easy since far less friction is involved.

Even if you dive in warm waters where wet suits aren't required, you'll still want to wear neoprene boots inside an open-heeled fin. This is because of the cushioning effect a boot has inside a strap-adjustable fin. Also, chances of chafing and blisters are virtually eliminated with boots inside a properly adjusted fin.

FINS FOR BARE OR HARD-TO-FIT FEET

If most of your diving will be in warm water where wet suits aren't needed, you may want the full-foot fin which encases your foot in a pocket shaped much like a low-slung tennis shoe. These fins are the hardest to fit because there's no means of adjustment. However, you can pick the size (5 to 7, 7 to 8½, 8½ to 10, and etc.) which most closely matches your foot. With extremely odd shaped

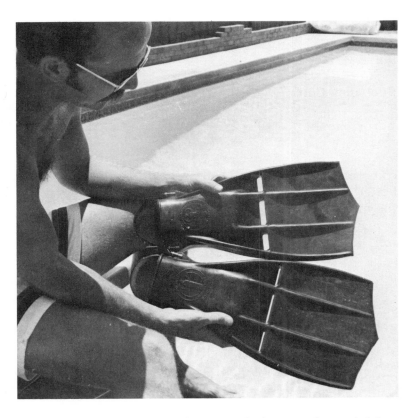

A satisfactory alternative choice for you as a beginner may be a scaled-down version of a larger vented fin. Most manufacturers now offer the smaller models which are very popular with women and student divers.

feet, the solution sometimes is to wear boots inside full-foot fins. Boots may be difficult to get in and out of the foot pocket and somewhat ugly to wear, but it is vital that you are comfortable when diving. Fins with a foot pocket also protect the bottoms of your feet from broken glass, coral, sea urchins, and similar hazards; so, of course, do boots.

One other type of fin seldom seen much anymore is the open-heel fin with a strap which is nonadjustable. These became popular with UDT divers during the Korean War but have largely given way to modern fins offering both an adjustable *and* replaceable strap.

FIN SIZE AND BEGINNING DIVERS

You'll see some extra-wide fins which are absolutely beautiful large things with nifty jet ports and vents all over the place. They remind one of an X-15 rocket plane. However, until your leg muscles get used to diving, you'll have trouble kicking the larger versions of these sexy looking monsters. Take a look instead at scaled-down versions of big, vented or long, stiff fins. Sure, the "big gun" fins are attractive and maybe the instructor does wear them, and maybe every other experienced diver you know wears them, but you're a beginning diver and there's a big difference.

Buoyancy Compensator (BC)

You should not scuba dive *or snorkel dive* unless you are wearing a buoyancy compensator. There are some newer, very good ones and there are still available for sale some comparatively poor, old-fashioned models. These, while better than nothing, cannot compare in performance to the many vests introduced since 1973.

A BC is worn for three reasons: neutral buoyancy control, flotation, and emergency flotation. Chapter Three explains how BC's extend a diver's vertical range, reduce his need to constantly fight negative/positive buoyancy, plus aid in resting anywhere, any time, especially at the surface. Now we'll study a little more about BC's and their great impact upon you as a sport diver.

In the days before BC's, divers counteracted wet suit buoyancy by wearing weights. These weights would typically equal in negative buoyancy the positive buoyancy caused by nitrogen bubbles trapped in the wet suit material at a given depth. This used to be the only method of buoyancy control that would cause weightlessness.

The problem, however, was that as a diver descended, the increased water pressure compressed his wet suit and reduced the volume of the neoprene material. Thus, at 33 feet down his wet suit offered much less buoyancy than it had provided at the surface. At 33 feet down the pressure on the wet suit is *twice* what it was at the surface.

Whereas at 33 feet down the wet suit gas has given up much of its *positive* buoyancy power, the weight belt continues to have approximately its original *negative* buoyancy power.

What this negative buoyancy meant to a diver in the days before BC's were widely used, was that at greater depths he'd constantly have a tendency to sink. He could always remedy this by swimming upwards a bit as he traveled along, but naturally this was tiring; it was somewhat like carrying around a stone. At 66 feet down—or three times atmospheric pressure—even more of a "sinking" problem would exist, requiring constant swimming "upwards."

For the most comfortable fit, always adjust a vest while it's fully inflated. This is when the buddy system comes in handy—Kathy Cully helps Gloria Koelzer tighten straps.

The point of all this discussion on pressure at different depths is to make you aware that when you dive with wet suit and weight belt, the increased pressure makes a diver become heavier as he goes deeper, which means he'll sink. And if the wet suit and belt are the only devices he's relying on for buoyancy control, he'll have a better chance of encountering problems than would a diver wearing a BC.

A buoyancy compensator vest allows you to "compensate" or make up for the trapped gas in your wet suit which has been reduced in volume due to pressure. With a BC you can control "sinking" and "rising" anytime. More importantly, you can stay virtually weightless during almost every minute of every dive.

Believe it or not, scuba divers went fifteen years or so before discovering the value of using an inflatable vest for buoyancy control. Why did they decide to use BC's? The primary reason was to BE COMFORTABLE IN THE WATER. The second reason was safety.

BC's all work basically the same way from a buoyancy control standpoint. They can be used to increase buoyancy when you're sinking and decrease buoyancy when you're rising. Listed below are considerations regarding selection of your BC.

SIZE

A good BC should have enough air volume capacity in pounds to equal, or better yet, exceed the poundage you'll carry on your weight belt when diving with a wet suit. This is only a rule of thumb, but a vest equalling or exceeding in flotation ability a diver's weight belt in poundage should easily hold his head out of the water at the surface when fully inflated. In addition, upon inflation it should provide any size body with plenty of lifting capacity even when wet suit volume is compressed at depth.

LET AN EXPERT HELP

When you visit a dive store to purchase your first BC, you'd be wise to arrange to meet your instructor there or perhaps pick him up on the way. Your BC will be the most valuable piece of diving gear you'll ever own so let an expert help you choose one. Chances are the instructor will advise you, as a beginner, to buy an intermediate sized vest of about 20-40 pounds air capacity. Such a vest is usually low-profile enough to reduce drag when snorkel diving, yet large enough for controlled, emergency ascents from scuba diving depths.

The reason your instructor may dissuade you, as a be-

The correct size vest for you equals or exceeds in air volume pounds the pounds you will carry on a weight belt when you scuba dive.

ginner, from buying an extra large 40-50 pound plus BC is that a vest of such size can, in certain emergencies which require the dropping of your weight belt, lead you to make an uncontrolled, too fast ascent which might result in a case of the bends or lung overexpansion at the surface. On the other hand, some of the newer, big vests have an "emergency dump valve" designed to help eliminate this potential problem.

FOUR KEY POINTS ABOUT BC USE

(1) When you're using an almost fully inflated BC to help you carry a heavy bag or other object, be sure to begin deflating the vest *immediately* should you release the heavy object.

(2) Whenever you have a nearly full vest and face an emergency which would normally dictate dropping your weight belt, start to dump air the very second you finish ditching your weight belt. Dumping air at depth *before* it expands just might make the difference between a safe controlled ascent and one that is dangerous and uncontrolled.

(3) Never overweight yourself. If you're certain you'll

Some larger volume BC's come equipped with an "emergency dump valve" which lets you reduce air volume more quickly during ascents. As Barb Steiner pulls the activator cord, large volumes of air escape from the valve.

be diving deeper than normal, remove some weights from your belt before entering the water. Otherwise, you'll create a potentially dangerous situation by relying too much on a high volume vest that could make you ascend like a rocket soon after dropping your weight belt.

(4) As a beginner, you might be better off with a medium volume BC for the first year or so. However, if you should buy a large volume vest, try to find one with an "emergency dump valve." This device, activated by a pull string, allows you to vent off vest air through an orifice in addition to the one on the BC mouthpiece. This feature probably doubles the rate of deflation.

EMERGENCY INFLATION DEVICE

Your instructor will probably insist that you buy a vest featuring emergency inflation capability. Such vests have attached to them either a CO_2 cartridge or a small compressed air bottle. The most popular is the CO_2 cartridge type.

This vest is swiftly inflated with CO_2 gas when a string is pulled. The string attaches to a firing mechanism which pierces a screwed-in CO_2 cartridge. Within seconds, the gas vents into the vest and provides instant buoyancy. The advantage here is that if you're somehow unable to gain positive buoyancy orally when you need it fast, it's always available to you by simply pulling a string.

Choosing Scuba Equipment   51

BC INFLATOR VALVE

Most quality BC's today can be converted so they inflate directly from the air supply system. This is done through means of a hose accessory which hooks directly to the intermediate pressure port on the first stage of the scuba regulator. As you need positive buoyancy, you simply depress a thumb valve and air enters the vest until the valve is released. Such a vest typically also inflates orally or, in emergency, by CO_2. Often, you can buy a vest with this inflator valve option included as part of the package. Doing this at the start will save you about $40 which is the average retail price to have a vest inflator installed.

Ideally, however, you should begin your instruction without actually using this advantage so you'll learn to always be comfortable *orally* inflating a vest. Remember, vest inflator valves are fine so long as there's air left in your tank to use. When the air is gone, you'll have to know how to inflate the vest orally anyway, or else trigger the one shot CO_2 gas cartridge.

Most air in a BC should be carried over your chest and abdomen, with the least amount in the neck area.

Ideally, a good BC turns you face up in the water whenever it's fully inflated, as demonstrated by Carol Raymond.

CONSTRUCTION

Have your instructor advise you on what constitutes a well-constructed BC. Ideally, however, it offers the following features:

(1) A three-dimensional shape which places most air volume around the chest and waist, with minimum inflation in the neck area for maximum comfort. Straps securing the vest to the body should not become uncomfortably tight at near-full inflation.

(2) The vest should be designed so that, if inflated, it turns you face up in the water if you're unconscious. Query the dive store owner or your instuctor carefully about this feature.

(3) The outside fabric should be both abrasion- and puncture-resistant, for example: heavyweight 14-gauge nylon with polyurethane backing. Some of the better vests feature a separate inside bag for actually holding the air. This bag should also be highly resistant to puncture and tearing. Seams should be doubly bonded or otherwise firmly laminated. The air bag itself should be of a durable material of at least 10-20 mil thick polyurethane or the equivalent.

(4) The inflator hose should be of a large diameter and fit as high as possible on the vest body near the neck area, with a push-button oral inflation valve and a mouthpiece designed to pass in and out of your mouth very quickly.

(5) The metal part of the CO_2 detonator mechanism should be of a highly corrosion-resistant material. The mechanism should have an easily accessible pull string of material not likely to rot. Ideally, the knob at the end of the string is large enough to be quickly located and grasped, even with gloves on, under emergency conditions. If the vest has an "emergency dump valve" string, this should be easily distinguishable, due to location, from the CO_2 activator string.

(6) The waist and crotch straps should be of a dense, synthetic long-lasting material and have adjusting buckles and hook-ups not likely to slip or release under extreme stress.

(7) The vest must have an "over-pressure" relief valve which is largely tamperproof. This valve, primarily to keep a vest from bursting, should be located low on the vest body so that, in case of failure, air will still remain trapped above it. (Vests with emergency dump valves are exempt here, their combination over-pressure relief/ dump valve may be located higher.) An over-pressure relief valve will usually vent air from the vest when the

While BC inflator hoses come in assorted shapes, what counts is how easily and quickly they can be activated to inflate a vest orally.

Left: The BC's CO_2 cartridge and firing mechanism should be checked for corrosion and proper operation prior to each dive.

Below: Ideally, an over-pressure relief valve is located low on the BC body. Directly to the right is the BC's CO_2 bottle, screwed into its trigger mechanism.

average internal pressure becomes higher by a few pounds than the external pressure.

(8) Vests available with a dump valve have two main advantages: (a) they allow for easy venting while ascending/descending during the course of the dive; (b) they help eliminate the danger of an uncontrolled ascent by providing a large-volume dump valve in addition to the venting ability of the inflator hose. It is possible for an experienced diver to deflate some of the 50 pound-plus vests from maximum inflation to empty in only a few seconds.

BUOYANCY COMPENSATOR PACKS

Many major manufacturers of professional quality diving equipment now offer an integrated buoyancy compensator pack. This unit consists of a BC hooked directly to a tank backpack. Typically, the pack eliminates the need to don a BC and, in some cases, even a weight belt. Some packs are designed to offset natural positive buoyancy, or that gained from a wet suit, by storing weight in a compartment behind the diver. Supposedly, you can "drop" your weight simply by pulling a cord and letting the weight fall out.

CONS

Investigate the value of such packs carefully before investing in one. They can present problems to a beginner because:

(1) They provide flotation *behind* you, not *below* you, thus the chest rests lower in the water. This makes breathing through a snorkel more difficult since the water pressure around your chest presses in harder against your lungs.

(2) Typically, the tank mounts in the middle of the surrounding inflatable vest. This makes such packs nearly twice as wide as even a big volume BC, thus their size tends to pitch you around more in the surf, currents, and rough seas. When inflated, their size also causes a considerable amount of needless drag, unless the entire rig is removed and the diver lies atop it.

Underwater, the BC's over-pressure relief valve vents air so the vest cannot explode.

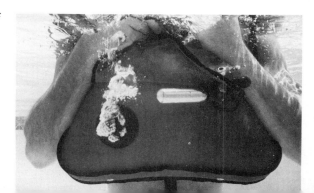

(3) It's possible the weight-dropping mechanism will fail—this has been known to happen.

(4) Such packs will not float an unconscious diver in a good face-up position. The flotation point on the best of them brings the head sideways to the water so that a person rides with chin submerged. Under ideal, glassy surface conditions, they might be OK. However, the ocean seldom cooperates.

PROS

Once you're underwater, BC packs are quite easy to use. At depth, it's far more comfortable not having a bulge on your chest and stomach which sometimes obscures downward vision. Used with a vest inflator valve, these packs provide excellent buoyancy compensation at depth with minimal effort. Most, however, lack the safety feature of a CO_2 cartridge detonator which might come in handy one day during an emergency. Still, there are experienced divers who consider the wearing of *separate* vests, tanks, backpacks, and weight belts a hassle compared to strapping on one unit which "does it all."

For you, as a beginning diver, these buoyancy compensator packs are not recommended unless you have successfully completed the appropriate course or have gained the permission of your instructor. Once you're certified and have made 20 or 30 dives, you may then want to consider this sort of buoyancy compensator pack.

In summary, the equipment needed to snorkel dive includes a good mask, snorkel, fins, and BC. Seek expert advice when choosing these, and save your sales receipt for each item. After all, masks have been known to leak, fins to rip, snorkels to crack, and BC's to spring holes. Should your basic snorkel diving equipment be faulty, the receipt will help guarantee replacement at no additional cost.

Remember one key point. *Anyone* can buy the snorkel diving gear described above. Even persons who should not be taking a diving course due to their physical or mental condition. Chapter 6 explains how to get yourself in shape to use this basic gear and qualify for a basic scuba certification course.

6 Snorkeling—The Basic Skills

Typically, most persons have their first exposure to snorkel diving as part of their basic scuba certification course. But you, thinking ahead logically, know that if prior to the course you can become familiar with using snorkeling gear, that part of the course will become considerably easier for you. So it makes a lot of sense to spend a few hours working out with your mask, snorkel, and BC in a private pool between the time you buy the gear and the time the instructor asks you to use it in your course.

However, before you start putting on equipment and snorkeling around the pool, remember one thing. Your ultimate objective in performing these exercises is to one day become a competent snorkel diver in open water. You begin practicing in a pool because it is a relatively safe, controlled environment for you, one in which *you already feel comfortable.* The ideal is for this comfort level to follow you into open water snorkel diving during a course and later into scuba diving you'll do your entire life long.

The exercises here are presented only to *prepare* you better for a basic skin diving or basic scuba diving certification course, though through much practice you will also likely become a very accomplished snorkeler in pools. If that lofty ambition is your ultimate skindiving goal, then you can master the pool environment quite easily by following the steps outlined for you here.

Never take these pool skills into open water without an instructor's guidance. In the lake, quarry, or ocean you can't hang an elbow over a handy pool edge every time you want to rest. So you might begin avoiding that practice in your pool exercises right from the start. Tread water instead.

One other point. Unless you've *already completed* a basic scuba course, never ever take it upon yourself to use any kind of scuba tank or regulator in a pool. Under certain conditions, such as a rapid ascent to the surface with lungs full from a breath taken off compressed air at the pool bottom, it's possible to suffer an air embolism using scuba in water as shallow as seven feet. Until you're a genuine card-carrying, certified scuba diver, leave scuba alone when the instructor's not around. Now that we've covered the cautions, let's begin learning how to get ready for the certification course.

Physical Fitness

Because using your head is 60 percent of diving, you'll be very smart to have a complete physical exam before spending much time even at the deep end of a pool. This exam is highly recommended, if not required, by most certifying organizations, as a prerequisite to taking a course. Since you're smart, you'll indeed have this medical examination and there's no better time than right away. The reason you'll do this is that first off you probably haven't had a physical exam for some time and thus should have one anyway and, second, there may be things wrong with you right now that could either prevent or significantly modify the extent of your diving. If you dive without knowledge of such things, you cease being a smart diver.

It's a safe statement that most doctors will not know much about the physics and physiology of diving unless they are either divers themselves or regularly treat divers. What you want is a doctor who knows how to examine you for things which might cause problems in the water. Finding such a doctor is quite easy. Simply use the phone book to check these classifications in the yellow pages: Divers, Divers' Equipment and Supplies, Skin Diving Equipment, and Skin Diving Instruction. Within a few calls you'll obtain the name of a doctor who knows how to evaluate you as a prospective diver.

If for some reason such a doctor cannot be located, or you must wait nearly forever for an appointment, your family or personal doctor will do, providing, of course, he knows what to check you for. The major certifying organizations, plus most dive stores, have medical examination forms which outline for the doctor what he must do. Obtain such a form and have the doctor follow its instructions. A sample medical form appears in the Appendix.

The physical prerequisites to diving typically read as follows:

(a) Free of cardiovascular and respiratory disease, with good exercise tolerance, no asthma, etc. (chest x-ray strongly recommended).

(b) Ability to equalize pressure in all body air spaces, no ear and sinus pathology/lung disease.

(c) Free of momentary impairment of consciousness, syncope, epileptic episodes, diabetic problems.

Mental Fitness

Evaluate *yourself* honestly in the mental category. If you are a true klutz on the land, always dropping things and stumbling, or making mistakes which injure yourself, chances are you'll be the same underwater. It is particularly important, however, that you can control your emotions under severe stress. *And only you know the real answer to how emotionally stable you are.* And, frankly, even you don't know.

If you have a history of mental problems, have neurotic trends, are reckless or accident-prone or panic easily, maybe diving is not for you. On the other hand, in some cases it could be therapeutic for you. If you can't judge for yourself, discuss your concern with a psychiatrist or doctor who's familiar with the physical *and* mental aspects of diving. Since the key to safe, enjoyable diving is to be COMFORTABLE IN THE WATER, you might have problems reaching this goal unless you are quite capable of understanding and controlling your emotions.

Swimming Ability and Watermanship

Part of being a smart diver is always staying in good physical condition. It is more important to develop overall endurance than it is to build sheer physical strength. You may have to swim against currents or through surf lines during a dive and both activities may extend for prolonged periods. In addition, you may one day need reserve energy to save yourself or someone else. Obviously, that's when proper conditioning and endurance are vital.

So, there are very good reasons why you must exhibit a certain degree of endurance before a diving instructor will admit you to his class. Actually, the requirements *sound* much harder than they really are. Chances are you couldn't do some of the exercises right now in a swimming pool. But after a week or two of practice, you can probably handle them all with plenty of energy to spare.

Most major certifying agencies expect you to demonstrate the following minimum standards before you can enter their basic scuba *or* snorkel diving courses:

(1) Distance Swimming—220 yards.

(2) Underwater Swim—20 yards.

(3) Survival Swimming (tread, bob, float, and drownproofing for 10 minutes).

Each certifying organization may vary in its emphasis of certain skills but approximations of these minimum standards have been agreed upon by the major certifiers (NASDS, NAUI, PADI, YMCA) for basic scuba and skin diving courses.

You may think that you could never swim 220 yards, but you're wrong. What might be true is that you cannot swim this distance *right now*. However, you will swim this distance if:

(1) You tell yourself you will swim those distances.

(2) You practice swimming on a regular basis.

(3) You truly want to learn scuba diving.

The way to qualify for the swimming part of a scuba certification course is to build your skills *gradually*. The place to practice, as mentioned earlier, is in a pool, because there you're relatively safe and can feel comfortable. Particularly if you have someone in the pool practicing with you, or at least at poolside to encourage your efforts.

Building Swimming Skills

First, measure the pool's length so that you know how many yards it is. If it's 20 yards, you will have to swim that distance 11 times to equal 220 yards. If you think you're fairly rusty at swimming, do only one very slow lap, then stop to evaluate your breathing and heart beat. If you're not terribly winded, rest several minutes, then swim back to the other end of the pool. Rest, and again take time to evaluate your breathing rate, heart beat, plus take note of any tightness or cramping in your leg or arm muscles. If, after a few minutes everything seems okay, swim very slowly to the other end of the pool. Rest again.

Swimming very slowly is stressed for this reason: Due to the drag of the water you displace with your body, it requires about four times the physical effort simply to double your swimming speed. Thus, going slowly conserves your energy which you can then use for making more, but slower, laps. On your first day of practice, swim three or four slow laps, then relax for half an hour or so. After a while, reenter the pool and swim some more, being sure to think only of doing one lap at a time. If you

As you begin your practice of basic swimming skills, enter the pool from the shallow end, without equipment, and concentrate on building endurance.

Swim slowly to conserve energy. It takes four times the energy simply to double your speed in water.

get very tired, stop. You can always continue the next day. Remember, too, that if you're not used to strenuous exercise, overexertion places a great burden on your heart, regardless of whether you're 15 or 50 years old. So take it easy the first few days. Your goal is to build your swimming endurance progressively, not to become an accomplished swimmer in a few days or even one week.

If you practice daily or every other day, and go very slowly, you'll soon be swimming 220 yards without stopping. Later, when you build your endurance sufficiently, you'll find you can swim even farther.

You can relax tightening muscles and eliminate danger of cramps by alternating strokes as you swim along on your way to reaching 220 yards. It is not important what kinds of strokes you use in this swim; only that you do swim the distance. By pacing yourself and alternating strokes, you can eventually swim the entire 220 yards and more.

During the certification course you'll also be expected to swim *underwater* for 20 yards without fins. Begin practicing for this by swimming across the *narrow* width of the

Your goal for scuba course entry is to swim 220 yards comfortably without stopping. In long-distance swimming the head should be supported by the water except during a breath. Then the head is turned only slightly to the side, as demonstrated by Barb Steiner.

pool at about a 4-foot depth. A rhythmic combination breast stroke and frog kick, followed by a short glide, will probably serve you best. Remember always that it takes about four times the energy to simply double your speed in the water. So go along first at a steady but slow rate.

You may doubt that you can hold your breath long enough to swim underwater for 20 yards, but as you practice, you'll be able to cover this distance in less than thirty seconds, even with the exertion required. Chances are you can hold your breath for thirty seconds right now as you sit there reading, if you first inhale quite deeply.

Watermanship takes practice. Your swimming must eventually become rhythmical. It would be good to read a book on basic swimming before you start precourse training. Better yet, enroll in a basic swimming refresher course at a recreation department or Y in your area.

Don't ever become discouraged, even after your first week of swimming. Typically, you'll find that after your second and third practice sessions, you'll doubt you'll ever be able to swim that 220 yards. But from the third workout on, you can expect big improvements every session, in rhythm, endurance, and even speed. This is because your muscles are adapting to the new demands upon them. Also, at this stage, you're already starting to relax, to become MORE COMFORTABLE IN THE WATER.

Getting To Know Your Skin Diving Gear

After you're finally swimming distances which will qualify you for a basic scuba diving course, or even as you're practicing, you should begin getting used to your mask, snorkel, fins, and BC. This is best done first at the shallow end of a pool. Ideally, use a private pool for this purpose. If this is not possible, try to get permission from the management of a public pool to practice early in the morning before regular hours. It's possible that a pool contractor would allow you use of a demonstrator model after business hours if all else fails. In any event, you shouldn't try any kind of diving in any open water, such as a lake, quarry, or ocean, until you're quite comfortable with your gear and have completed a basic diving course. And *never, never* go in a pool alone. Have someone watching who could rescue you immediately.

Prewater Check of Buoyancy Compensator

Because you've likely chosen a *heated* pool, you'll not be wearing a wet suit for this practice. So your buoyancy compensator will fit directly against your skin. However, before you put on the vest, examine it carefully. Expose the part of the vest, typically the pocket, covering the CO_2 cylinder and trigger mechanism. (While they are not discussed here, there are many very good vests made without CO_2 cylinders. They are usually of a lower volume, lower profile than a BC and often have very small oral inflation tubes compared with BC hoses. Vests have been used for years in diving and indeed do an adequate job, though perhaps less comfortable than a BC. For convenience, the terms BC and vest have been used interchangeably throughout this book.) Unscrew the CO_2 cylinder and check the threads and its socket for signs of corrosion. Carefully inspect the firing pin to see that it extends far enough to fire a fully screwed-in cartridge. Inspect the firing pin's lever mechanism, its housing, and the string attached to the lever. Be sure the string is new

Before entering the pool, practice inflating and deflating the BC until you can easily perform all the functions with your eyes closed.

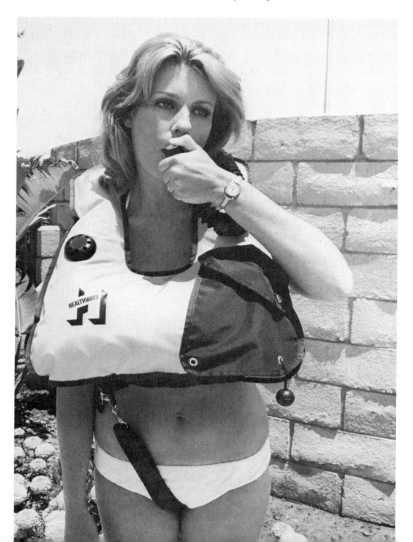

and not rotted or partially cut. Hold the lever tightly up inside its housing and tug hard on the string. That string should be checked before and after every dive, whether in a pool or in open water. That's because if that basic little string ever comes unknotted, broken, or lost, you'll probably be unable to discharge the CO_2 cartridge into your vest. Typically, the cartridge is used only in an emergency—when *everything* must work perfectly, including you. So it is not simply for drill that you inspect the string now and before each use of a BC for the rest of your life.

When you've finished the inspection, make sure the firing pin lever is back up flush inside its housing, then screw the cartridge back in firmly.

Stand on the pool deck and adjust the BC crotch and waist straps according to the manufacturer's instruction booklet or as follows: The vest crotch strap should be comfortably snug. This is so the vest will not rise up against your chin or mask when inflated. The waist strap should also be snug but not tight. Having this strap too loose will allow the vest to move away from you and increase water drag. Having the strap tight may cause discomfort.

Now bend down and wash off the vest mouthpiece in the pool. This will make it more slippery and help you fit it into your mouth the first time. Depress the plunger, or other valve device, at the end of the hose one time and release it. Look inside the mouthpiece/valve and notice how it works. You'll see that when you depress the plunger the hose passage opens, and when you release the plunger the passage closes. Now, with the fingers of your left hand on the plunger, place the hose mouthpiece in your mouth. Don't bite it. Hold it gently there with your hand. Take a deep breath and depress the plunger. Blow half a big breath into the hose. Release the plunger and take another big breath. Again, blow half or two thirds of the breath into the hose and again release the plunger. Repeat these steps until the vest is full. You'll notice that as the vest builds up internal pressure, it will expel air the instant you stop exhaling unless you release the plunger.

After the vest is very full and you can blow in no more air, note whether or not the crotch and waist straps have gotten uncomfortably tight. If they have, readjust them.

Now, hold up the hose with your left arm and depress the plunger. Hold it down until the vest seems to have exhausted itself. Place your right arm over the bottom of the vest and press against yourself. You'll notice that this action forces a fair amount of tidal air from the vest. There may be a time later on in your diving experience when this "sandwich technique" of total vest deflation may help you reduce unwanted buoyancy more quickly. Repeat the inflation/deflation process enough times so you're both sure about how this is done and can find the hose mouthpiece quickly, even when it's dangling out of sight.

Water Practice with a Buoyancy Compensator

Leave your mask, snorkel, and fins on the pool edge near the stairs at the shallow end. Your concentration should be upon your vest.

Enter the water to waist depth. Now, inflate the vest half full and then lean slightly forward on it. Notice how it buoys you up and lifts your feet. Let your legs rise from the pool bottom, now float atop the vest. Stay in the same depth for a while and float around this way until you find it easy using arms and legs to balance yourself atop the water. Next, roll over on your back and float until you've mastered this inflated challenge to your balance.

Venture now into chest-high water. On the way, fully inflate your vest, but be sure your feet can still touch the bottom. Take the hose and, with your left hand held higher than the vest, activate the plunger to release a small amount of air. Check to be sure you can still touch bottom, back up if necessary, then depress the plunger again. Flex your knees and sink until the water is just under your chin. If you now extend the hose straight up, chances are the water pressure will exhaust virtually all the air from the vest. If you were on a real dive, you'd be either neutrally or just negatively buoyant now and you could swim to the bottom. In fact, that is the next exercise.

Duck underwater and swim that way back to the shallow end of the pool. (Note how a deflated vest offers little drag.) Stand up at the 3-foot level and inflate the vest about half full. Now swim out to a depth where you can still touch bottom and spend the next few minutes swimming back and forth across the narrow end of the pool. Stop occasionally, with your feet off the bottom and the vest supporting you, and practice blowing air in and venting it out of the vest. When you feel *comfortable* enough, go down to the deep end and back with the vest inflated. Try this several times, then return to the shallow end and deflate the vest.

Don't be alarmed if you notice that some water has gotten inside your BC. This is natural and cannot be avoided. However, if it becomes quite full of water (which is unlikely), remove the vest on the pool deck, inflate it about a third full, and simply pour and squeeze the water out after inverting the vest and the valve. When you're done practicing for the day, run *fresh* water inside the vest through the inflator hose. Slosh the water around, then pour it out to cleanse pool chemicals from the BC. Finally, wash off the BC's exterior and all your other gear.

Mask

DEFOGGING

Keep your fins and snorkel where you can reach them at the pool edge near the steps or shallowest depth. Continue wearing your BC and take your mask in your hands. Now, quite unceremoniously and regardless of how crass it might seem to you or those watching, gather a mass of saliva in your mouth. Then spit it forcefully on the inside of your mask faceplate.

For best results, use your highest grade, stickiest saliva and deliver it with the finese and accuracy befitting a tobacco-chewing Lil' Abner mountain character. Diving is serious sport, so there is a very good reason for this otherwise socially unacceptable exercise! The saliva keeps your mask from fogging up, and because of this you'll be able to see better.

The last time I forgot this little ceremony, I was 80 feet down on a colorful reef absolutely jammed with marine life just off Diamond Head in Hawaii. Because I'd performed the spitting ritual haphazardly without its proper attention before leaving the boat, I was forced to remove my fogged-up mask at depth, rub the lenses vigorously with my fingertips, then put the mask back on and clear it of water. Fortunately, the mask stayed clear afterwards.

While the process of removing a mask and defogging it underwater is easy enough for an experienced diver, to do so is nonetheless highly annoying, in addition, my eyes burned slightly for the rest of the dive from something in the water.

Had the fogging not disappeared, I'd have had to return to the surface, do my spitting and rubbing act, then return to the reef where I'd have surely missed an incredible and rarely seen brief fight three of us witnessed between a moray eel and a rather large octopus which seemed to have an unlimited ink supply.

Incidentally, your mask tends to fog up because the air it traps next to your face becomes heated by expiration from your nostrils and your facial warmth. Since this air inside the mask is warmer than the water on the outside

(a) At waist depth, inflate the vest, lift your legs, and let the BC support you.

(b) Raise the inflator hose above the vest and depress the plunger to vent air.

(c) Let the rising water completely vent the BC as you sink under the surface.

(d) Knowledge of how to operate a BC properly will be stressed in your basic scuba certification course.

(e) Practice swimming with your BC until you're used to balancing yourself on it.

You begin to fog-proof a mask by first spitting into it. After spitting onto both sides of the face plate, rub the saliva into the glass. Then rinse by immersing the entire mask once in the water.

of the glass faceplate, the heated air is humidified and forms water droplets inside the faceplate. Saliva, however, contains a wetting agent which keeps the water beads to a smaller size. As a result, they simply form a smooth film which you'll never see while diving because it is transparent.

Once you've thoroughly rubbed the inside of the lens with saliva, immerse the mask completely in the pool water just once and quickly remove it. Then shake out any water drops remaining.

DONNING A MASK

To put a mask on you *do not put the strap on first*. If you do, chances are you'll get a leaky seal due to bending a feather edge inward or trapping a few strands of hair. Move the strap above the lens and fit the mask tightly against your face until it can be held there by inhaling through your nose. Only then do you transfer the strap up and over to the back of your head.

You should already have the strap adjusted so it is simply "snug." On a tightness scale of 1-10, the strap should ideally rate a 5 or 6 at the most. Remember, the strap does not seal the mask. The fit does. A tight strap can cause a headache. Getting a headache is inconsistent with being COMFORTABLE IN THE WATER. And when you're uncomfortable, you should end the dive, or even an equipment familiarization session in a pool.

SEEING WITH A MASK

With the mask in place, enter the shallow end of the pool. Bend down so your mask is underwater and look at your feet. You'll see they appear about 25 percent larger to you. Reach down to grab a big toe and you'll find it appears bigger and closer than it really is. This phenomenon is natural with a diving mask.

Such magnification is caused by light passing first through water, then through a glass lens, through the air pocket of your mask, then through your eyes. In this journey, the light bends, it is refracted. Also, such enlargement cuts down the field of vision the same as it would if you were looking through a telescope which also enlarges objects. Fortunately, you quickly adjust to this tunnel vision deception and, after a while, are largely unaware that while underwater your vision has "improved" by about 25 percent.

Swim underwater around the shallow end of the pool getting used to having your mask on. Avoid the deep end of the pool for a while. Before you venture there, the next task is to become familiar with clearing the mask of water.

WATER IN A MASK

Sooner or later in your future scuba diving, your mask will leak or be dislodged so that water enters to interfere with your vision, irritate your eyes, or slosh in an annoying fashion against your nostrils. This, too, is certainly not conducive to being COMFORTABLE IN THE WATER. So the

(a) Get used to a mask slowly. Begin by standing waist deep in water and studying how your feet on the pool bottom look about 25 percent larger to you through a mask.

goal is to expel the nuisance water quickly in a manner not disruptive to the dive and not wasting time ascending to the surface.

Above water, clearing a flooded mask is simple. You just break the mask's seal at its lowest point and the water pours out. Underwater, with practice, the task is almost as simple. In your diving to come, you will perform mask clearing hundreds of times automatically and probably forget that you are even doing it.

You begin practicing mask clearing by standing first waist deep in water with your mask properly sealed on your face. Next, bend down until the mask is totally underwater. Move the mask out slowly away from your face. Exhaling through your nose will help break the seal. Let the water completely fill the mask and when it's full, seal it back against your face.

Now, stand up straight and analyze what has changed now that your mask contains water. The biggest change is that you've lost your "window to the water," which was the air gap between your eyes and the glass faceplate. Because this area is now filled with water, you see exactly the same as you do underwater without a mask. Everything is a blurry mass of shapes and forms. This is what will happen when your mask occasionally gets bumped aside underwater, or its seal leaks and good vision is lost or impaired during a dive.

You'll also notice how awkward it is initially to breathe through your mouth while your nose is submerged. You have to breathe carefully so water is not drawn up your nostrils. It should be particularly obvious to you by this time that having a flooded mask is by no means at all consistent with BEING COMFORTABLE IN THE WATER. During your scuba certification course, your mask will be intentionally flooded by you and then cleared many times as a basic exercise. This is done in a course so you'll become accustomed to seeing and breathing temporarily this troublesome way without panic until you can correct the problem.

The solution to a flooded mask is to eliminate the water quickly and continue the dive. Fortunately, this is quite easily done once you know how. And it's far easier to do while wearing scuba than it is while snorkel diving. But because you'll be performing mask clearing with scuba during your course, it's of value to you to become familiar with the technique now.

Without scuba, mask clearing is harder since the air exhaled through your nostrils to clear your mask cannot be replaced in your lungs by inhaling from a constant

(b) Move the mask away from your face and let it fill with water. Then reseal it with the water trapped inside.

(c) Stand and observe how uncomfortable you feel with a mask full of water. Try breathing through your mouth while your nose is surrounded by water.

scuba air supply. It simply diminishes the air remaining from your last breath.

As you *stand* there in the pool with your mask full of water against your face, tip your head back slightly. Take your hand and pull the *bottom* of the mask away from your face until the mask seal releases below your nose. Now simply let the water completely drain out, then reseal the mask. This is the way you clear a flooded mask at the surface. The process is basically the same at depth except that you'll be surrounded by water which is trying to enter your mask. It tries to enter the mask because it's heavier than air. On the surface, all that's trying to enter

(d) Tip the bottom of the mask away from your face and let the water pour out. The mask shown has prescription-ground lenses affixed inside. These lenses are visible in this view of Harold Boehm.

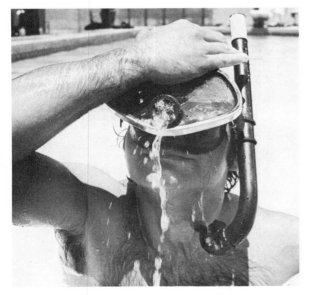

(e) Refill the mask, then press in against the top. Exhale through your nose. Doing so forces water out the face seal above your lip or, in the example shown here, out through a one-way purge valve located in the mask.

your mask is relatively light air and that's exactly what you want.

After you've let the water pour out the bottom of your mask, drop your head under the surface again and refill the mask with water. Be sure the mask reseals against your face then stand up. This time, rather than pour the water out the bottom as you did before, try the following: press firmly against the top of the mask and look upwards. Then exhale through your nose. You'll find that the water is automatically forced out the bottom seal of the mask as soon as the air displaces it. If your mask has a purge valve, be sure to look down when exhaling so the valve is at the lowest point on the mask.

CLEARING A MASK

Underwater, you expel water from a flooded mask and replace it with air the same way—by exhaling through your nose. This exhaled air enters the mask at a higher pressure than the water. Thus it forces the water to, in effect, *pour* out of the lowest part of the mask the same way it did above the surface. It is essential to perfect this skill later with scuba and here's how you practice it on your own before beginning a scuba course.

Go to the side of the pool where the water is about shoulder height. Stand with your mask sealed and, if you like, your feet on the bottom of the pool. Put your left hand against either side of the mask until water begins entering through the other side. Let the mask fill up so the water is over your eyes. Then let go of the mask. It should automatically reseal.

Because this is your first time trying this, lift your head up out of the water and breathe. Take a big breath through your mouth and push yourself back under. Be sure your head is completely underwater. *Tilt your head back so you're looking at the water's surface* and, with one hand, press firmly inward against the *top* of your mask's faceplate. While you're still maintaining hand pressure, breathe firmly through your nose and *into* the mask. If your mask is a low-volume one, this action should force all the water out below your nose so you can see clearly again. If some water still remains, exhale a little more air, only do it a bit more sharply this time.

If your mask is of a large volume (usually having a single oval lens instead of two), it will require more exhalation to clear. In this case, and because this should be a comfortable exercise, you may want to first clear out just part of the water, rise up for a big breath, then go under again, repeating this process several times until the mask is empty of water. However, perhaps you'd be better off going out and buying a smaller volume mask which clears more easily.

One of the keys to clearing a mask successfully is this: Always make sure that the point where you press inwards is at the *uppermost* part of the mask, closest to the surface. In addition, be sure this point is on a direct vertical line with the *lowest* part of the mask in the water. This is important because what really works for you when you breathe air into the mask is simple gravity. This gravity makes the displaced water inside the mask tend to "fall" downwards in a straight line, just as it does when you pour water out of any container above the surface. So it

1. Take a deep breath, drop under the surface, and fill the mask with water.

2. Look upwards, press against the top of the mask, and exhale through the nose. Note how the air is being forced out at the mask's lowest point.

3. If the mask does not completely empty of water on your first try, exhale again through your nose, making sure the bottom of your mask is the lowest point in the water.

Clearing water from a mask by forcing it out through a purge valve.

doesn't matter so much whether you press inwards on the mask at the top or the side. Just so long as that point is the highest vertical point on the mask at that moment. Another point: A very few masks will clear more easily from some point other than the bottom-most part. In a scuba course, the instructor, however, will teach you how to clear *your* particular mask in whatever way works best for you, and the mask you're using at the time. The technique outlined here is the way most nonpurge valve masks are cleared.

CLEARING THROUGH A PURGE VALVE

Many masks have a purge valve on the front which either extends through the glass faceplate or the rubber body. This valve lets water and air out but not in. Thus, when a mask floods, you simply hold it sealed against your face, ensure the purge valve is the lowest underwater point on the mask, and exhale through your nose. The water exits through this valve, rather than by passing under the tightest sealing part of the mask skirt. This mask, however, can cause problems especially if the valve fails and lets water in. It's just one more thing to worry about going wrong. If you should, for some reason, decide on a purge valve mask, be sure to get one with a very large diameter valve to allow rapid clearing with a minimum volume of air. There are some very excellent purge masks available, and some not so excellent ones. Therefore, you'd be wise to get an expert's advice before choosing one. Invariably, purge masks cost more. Also, a purge is not primarily a means to clear the entire mask of water but a device for expelling small amounts of water.

MASK SQUEEZE

As you venture underwater into deeper pool water, you'll notice that the mask presses in against your face.

Even at a few feet of depth, this "mask squeeze" becomes somewhat uncomfortable. At greater depths it can hurt your eyes. As usual in diving, there is a very simple solution. Just exhale a bit of air into the mask as you descend. This equalizes the lower pressure air trapped behind the faceplate with the higher pressure water on the other side of the faceplate. As soon as you do this, the squeezing will stop until you go deeper.

EQUALIZING EAR PRESSURE

Another uncomfortable sensation you will experience as you go deeper is a pressure in your ears. This is caused because the air in your middle ear and eustachian tube is usually at a lower pressure than the water on the outside of the eardrum. As you descend, this uncomfortable feeling is generally caused by a blockage in, or at the entrance to, the eustachian tube. The pressure differential naturally increases as you go deeper and the "heavier" water outside wants to displace the "lighter" air inside. As a result, the water presses harder and harder against the eardrum trying to get past it and fill the low-pressure area in your head.

Ultimately, this could lead to the eardrum stretching inwards until it broke. A ruptured eardrum is dangerous to a diver because when cold water enters the inner ear, equilibrium is lost, and usually one cannot easily distinguish between up and down. The solution is simply to wait for a few moments until the cold water in the ear warms up. Once this happens, equilibrium will be restored. Meanwhile, the diver can simply hold onto something, even himself, until balance returns.

To "equalize" ear pressure, your instructor will show you a number of techniques, which are thoroughly covered in texts used for scuba diving courses. Basically, they all do the same thing inside your head: force or allow air into a tube temporarily blocked by mucus. The result is that air at an already equalized pressure from the lungs enters the previously blocked tube, thus matching the water pressure on the outside of the eardrum. When this is done, the discomfort goes away unless further descent is made.

While you are practicing in a pool of less than a 10-foot depth, you will have little danger of rupturing an eardrum. To eliminate discomfort, try the following techniques for equalizing the ears.

● If your mask has finger pockets or a nose pocket, pinch your nose *shut* and try to blow moderately hard. You won't be able to, but the back pressure developed

Equalizing ear pressure by pinching the nose and trying to exhale through it.

You equalize ear pressure while wearing a purge-valve mask by pressing the mask in, closing off the valve, then exhaling through your nose. This equates pinching the nostrils shut.

may "clear" your ears. Never *force* your ears to equalize. If clearing does not come easily, rise to a shallower depth and try again. And never dive with a cold or sinus problem of any kind.

● If you find you have very little trouble in equalizing ear pressure, it may be enough for you simply to swallow or move your jaws a bit as you descend.

● If your mask has a purge valve *without* a nose pocket or equalizer where you can pinch your nose, you'll have to hold your hand over the valve so it can't vent air while you're pressing the entire mask against your face. This equates pinching your nose and blowing. If your purge-valve mask has a finger space for reaching the nose, the procedure is the same as for any mask.

● Much more can be said about equalizing mask and

ear pressure, but it has to do with the physiology and physics of diving—topics which your instructor is sure to cover in the course.

One final point about the ears. Never use ear plugs in skin or scuba diving. Increased water pressure can drive them into the outer ear canal and even *through* the eardrum. You can imagine how intensely painful this would be.

Fins

For some beginning divers, fins are the simplest to master of all the snorkel diving gear. Getting used to them is easier if you think of them simply as "bigger feet." To start your familiarization with fins, sit on the edge of the pool at the shallow end. You should be wearing your recently spit-upon and thus defogged mask, and your BC. Have your feet in the water and your fins on the pool deck beside you.

If your fins are open-heeled ones, you'll probably be

Remember, whether you wear full-foot or open-heeled fins, wetting both fins and feet makes "suiting-up" a lot easier.

Work both fins as one unit. They should barely clear each other when short, efficient flutter kicks are made.

wearing neoprene boots to prevent chafing. If your fins have a full-foot pocket, you'll likely be barefooted. In either case, be sure to wet both your fins and your feet or boots. Doing this helps reduce friction so the fins go on easily.

Put the fins on and push off into the water. Swim around the pool for a while, getting used to how the fins feel on your feet and how they easily double your swimming power. After about ten minutes of this, you should practice the two most basic fin strokes—the flutter kick and the scissors. First, however, keep in mind a few basic keys to effective finning:

● Keep your arms at your sides. Underwater they only create drag if used; not propulsion.

Keep knees as straight as possible for maximum power. End each stroke with a flip of the fin tip for even more efficient thrust.

Your fins should never break the surface when snorkeling. Forgetting this rule is a common error shared by nearly all beginning divers.

● Bend your knees only slightly. Keep them as straight as possible and let the fins and especially the "whip" of your fin tips do the work. Your knees create drag when bent, because each time a leg comes forward, it pushes *against* the water in a manner imparting *backwards* motion. Remember, always keep the knees semistraight and the arms at the sides for the most streamlined profile in the water.

● Keep your fins always totally submerged when swimming or snorkeling along the surface. Fins breaking the surface are losing power.

● Use your two fins as one unit. Keep your heels close enough together so they barely clear each other in passing up and down.

FLUTTER KICK

Even though it may be satisfying just to be able to swim more easily with fins than without, you should still strive to use them in the least tiring way. The best stroke for this is the flutter kick, in which the stroke length is only one to

These fins are too far apart for an effective flutter kick. A good stroke length is from 12-24 inches.

1.

2.

3.

4.

1. The restful scissors kick begins with the legs spreading apart.

2. The legs come forcefully together, giving strong forward thrust. Note that the stroke can be done on the right or left side and the snorkel will still remain above water.

3. The "rest" part of the stroke comes with a long graceful glide. Also, different leg muscles are used from those necessary in the flutter kick, so the two strokes can be alternated as needed.

4. After the glide, the fins spread wide again and the scissors kick is repeated.

two feet. Such a short stroke produces minimal drag and also takes advantage of a smartly executed "snap" of the flexible fin tips as your strokes reverse their direction.

Fins are a good example of Newton's third law of motion: "Every action is opposed by an equal and opposite reaction." In this case it is leg and ankle muscles versus water resistance.

SCISSORS KICK

This kick is often used as a resting stroke and as an alternate to the flutter kick. Sometimes, when you're on a long snorkel swim, your leg muscles grow tired and may start to tighten up. The scissors kick, much like a swimmer's side stroke, helps rest tired leg muscles and, allows you forward motion. It also offers the bonus of a relaxing *glide*. (In scuba diving underwater, the scissors kick is not necessarily done on the side as it is while snorkeling on the surface.)

To practice this kick, turn your body sideways on the surface and think of the way your legs move when you're towing a swimmer. The first few times you try the stroke, hold onto the edge of the pool with one arm, look back, and watch your fins move. Be sure to keep them totally underwater. As mentioned earlier, a fin that breaks the surface has cost you power and propulsion. This is because fins are designed to give thrust with both the downward *and* upwards stroke, and you lose part of that upward stroke when the fins aren't pushing against the water.

DOLPHIN KICK

In the certification course, your instructor will help you develop an efficient underwater kick called the "dolphin." In this, your fins and legs stay together and your whole body undulates in a wavelike movement which offers powerful propulsion with little drag. It is far easier to learn from a demonstration by a swimmer or illustrated through photos than by reading about it. The dolphin kick is only for *underwater* use. On the surface, it will only tend to push you beneath the water.

The Snorkel

Always attach the snorkel to the left side of the mask near your left ear. You do this so you always know where to find it, plus that way it's always on the opposite side from the mouthpiece part (second stage) of your single hose regulator when you begin using scuba gear.

ATTACHING AND ADJUSTING

To begin practice with your snorkel, you must first attach it to your mask. Do this by using the rubber snorkel "keeper" which was supplied by the manufacturer. These can be bought for a few cents in any dive store—it's a good idea to have a spare on hand. Slide one open end of

1. The dolphin kick begins with fins coming together, head down, and the body bent slightly at the waist.
2. As the fins finish their down stroke, the head and shoulders raise up and the back begins to arch slightly.
3. With back arched and head up, a new power stroke is ready to begin.
4. With the second power stroke finished, the back will arch and the fins will rise upwards again. Remember that in a dolphin kick, the head is up as the fins go up and down as the fins move down.

1.

2.

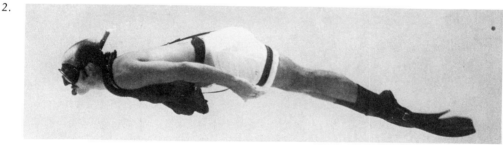

3.

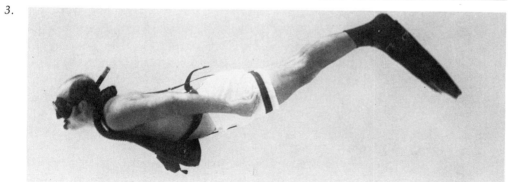

4.

A snorkel always fits onto the left side of the mask above the left shoulder.

the keeper just over the top of the snorkel, put in the mask strap, then slide the other keeper end over the tube.

You'll have to work the tight-fitting keeper and the encircled mask strap down the snorkel tube. It helps to wet the snorkel and keeper. When the snorkel's J is backwards and its mouthpiece ends up directly under your mask, you are close to the proper position.

For a final adjustment, put the mask on. Be sure the snorkel J extends far enough below the keeper so that the mouthpiece is in perfect alignment with the line of your closed mouth. You should be able to put the snorkel into your mouth *without* disturbing the seal of your mask or pulling against its strap.

Take the curved part of the snorkel in your left hand and move the mouthpiece upwards inside your mouth. With your teeth, grasp the two rubber bits lightly. Settle the larger ends of the bits behind your teeth and the wide flange between your gums and the inside of your lips. Readjust the snorkel where it hooks onto the mask. All you can hope to do at this stage of your experience is to get the snorkel adjusted so it doesn't break the face mask seal as it goes in and out of your mouth. After you've worn the snorkel for several sessions, you'll know far better exactly how it should be adjusted.

THE FIRST BREATH

To begin pool practice with the snorkel, it's best to leave your fins off for a while, since they'll make it harder for you to stand. Enter the water at the shallow end of the pool and proceed to waist depth. Practice breathing for a while through the snorkel while standing up. Then, bend down and place only your mask and face in the water. Reach up with your left hand to ensure the snorkel is fairly straight up. Then, study your feet for a while and continue breathing through the tube.

You'll find that you can feel the water pressure pressing up against the mask, even in a few inches of depth. You'll also notice that the mask seems to seal better because of this pressure. It'll seem awkward at first to breathe through your mouth only, but this sensation largely passes in an hour or so of snorkeling. Stay in this face down position for a while or, if your bent back begins to hurt, move to the side of the pool and hold onto the edge with both hands. Lift your legs up flat behind you and keep them floating just under the surface. You may have to kick slightly to stay level.

Always breathe *in* slowly and evenly. Breathing in slowly helps prevent sucking in any water which might enter the tube. Exhale forcefully to blow out water if it is present.

1. Get acquainted with a snorkel by breathing through it as you stand, head under, at the shallow end of a pool.

2. *Then, submerge and let water enter the tube. Still keeping face underwater, raise your head so the snorkel is out of water and blow the tube clear.*

BLAST CLEARING A SNORKEL

The next exercise is best done, once again, waist deep in water. Bend over as before with your mask totally submerged. Take a very large breath through the snorkel and hold the breath. Then slowly and deliberately immerse your entire head until you're sure the top of the snorkel is also underwater. Raise your head slowly so that the mask remains in the water but the snorkel top is out of the water. Now, exhale into the snorkel as forcefully and as *sharply* as is comfortable, making a loud "chu" sound.

After you've done this, breathe in through the snorkel very slowly, still keeping your face mask underwater. If you've completed this exercise correctly the first time, you now understand how the snorkel works. If you had problems, redo the exercise until you can blast clear the snorkel completely. It's natural for some water to enter the snorkel when you submerge, but because it enters above a column of air, it will not reach your mouth unless you inhale. Just don't inhale while underwater with a snorkel in your mouth.

At times, residual water remains after the first blast. This is particularly common in snorkels with sharp angles or flexible bellows where water can collect. That is why you always inhale slowly through a snorkel—so that this residual water is not "vacuumed" into your mouth and throat. Your first slow breath after blast clearing will tell you whether there's water in the tube. If there is, simply blast it out doubly hard with the next breath.

EXPANSION METHOD OF SNORKEL CLEARING

Later, while you are at the deep end of the pool, near the bottom, *look upwards* and release a breath of air into the snorkel tube. Keep your head up and rise towards the surface. While you ascend, the breath expands in the snorkel tube, driving out the water, thereby saving you the effort of blast clearing. Obviously, this particularly easy method of snorkel clearing works only while you're making an ascent.

SNORKELING AND SWIMMING

After you've gotten rather good at staying in one place and blast clearing a snorkel, put your fins on and swim across the narrowest width of the pool, making several shallow dives on the way and blast clearing the snorkel each time. Then try swimming the longest length of the pool the same way. Be sure as you dive down into the deeper water that you exhale a bit of air into the mask to avoid mask squeeze. Also, as you make deeper descents,

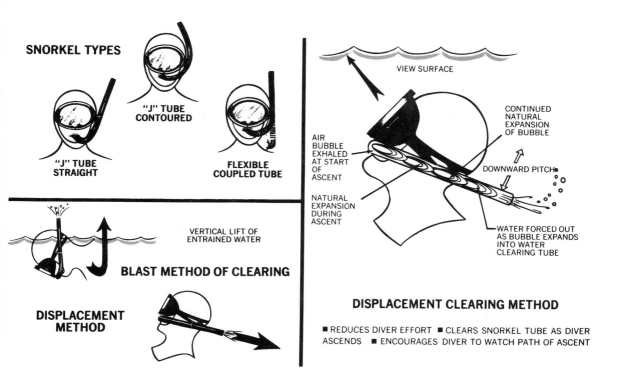

Expansion (displacement) method of clearing a snorkel.

Swim back and forth across the pool, breathing through the snorkel, then holding your breath and taking some shallow dives. Blast clear the snorkel at the surface but keep your face in the water.

you'll probably want to equalize the pressure in your ears by using one of the techniques discussed earlier. This is also the time to continue practicing the expansion method of snorkel clearing.

FLOODED MASK SNORKEL BREATHING

You should also learn how to breathe through your snorkel even when your mask is flooded. For this exercise return to waist-deep water and flood the mask. Keep your flooded mask underwater and breathe through the snorkel. Doing this will seem very uncomfortable, but it is important that you master this exercise now because later, when using scuba at depth, you'll occasionally be breathing through your mouth while your mask is flooded and your nose is in water. Spend some time on this exercise. You'll be expected to do it later in your diving course.

TESTING YOUR SNORKELING SKILLS

Here's a somewhat difficult exercise for you as a beginner—do it *only* after you feel you've really gotten the hang of snorkeling. First, be sure your buddy is watching you. Then take a deep breath and swim down to the drain hole in the deep part of the pool. Don't forget to equalize your ear pressure as you go down and exhale through your nose to avoid mask squeeze. At about the 9-foot depth, flood your mask by breaking the face seal. After the mask is flooded, tilt your head up, press the top part of the mask, and exhale through your nose. When you've cleared the mask of water, rise to the surface but keep your face in the water. Clear the snorkel by either the blast or expansion method, then breathe in slowly. Swim face down to the side of the pool, still breathing through the snorkel. Then get out of the pool and take a break, because if you can do that exercise perfectly, you are certainly serious about becoming a good student in your scuba certification course.

Practice these snorkeling exercises until each one is a "piece of cake" for you. The more difficult you make it for yourself during practice now, the easier time you'll have later during your certification course and your entire sport diving career.

7
Water
Entries

Up to this point in the exercises, you've probably entered the pool by walking down steps or by sitting on the pool edge then slipping into the shallow water. But in the scuba certification course you'll learn a variety of ways to enter an open-water environment such as a lake, quarry, or ocean.

The following advice is offered to prepare you for the water entries you'll find in the certification course:

- *Never make a headfirst dive while wearing a mask.*
- *Always know the approximate depth of the water you're entering.*
- Never *run and jump* into the water; either step in, slide in, fall in, or walk in.
- Never enter the water while alone. Always have someone watching you, at least, if not alongside you.
- Forget about appearances when you make water entries. Unlike competitive Olympic high-diving, big, noisy splashes upon entry are usually better in snorkel and scuba diving than are small, quiet ones.
- Always take a *deep* breath before making an entry.
- Keep your hand held tightly against your mask when making entries until you've returned to the surface.
- Always look up towards the surface when ascending to avoid objects above you.
- Always shuffle *backwards* with fins: Do not walk forward more than a *few* steps.

Front Entry or "Giant Stride"

To practice this most commonly used entry from a boat deck, dock, pool edge, or other relatively flat, stable surface, begin by standing near the deep end of the pool. You should wear your BC, mask, snorkel, and fins. Inflate your BC about three breaths' worth. Stand with your fins extending half over the pool edge and your weight on the back of your feet. Put an open hand over the front of your

A "Giant Stride" water entry

1. The giant stride begins by lifting one foot and simply stepping forward.

2. Forward momentum carries you well away from the pool edge by the time you hit the water.

3. A properly executed stride keeps your head from going under. Generally, the bigger splash you make the closer to the surface you'll remain.

1. *Harold Boehm shows proper form for a giant stride.*

2. *The spread-apart position of the legs helps retard downward motion.*

3. *Bringing the legs quickly together after entry also retards downward motion. Note that the head is still above water.*

4. *The bubbles show how the action of legs and fins coming together can quickly halt downward momentum after entry.*

5. *With the fins together, the diver's head is still above the surface. The advantage of the giant stride is the limited degree to which one becomes disoriented after hitting the water.*

mask and hold it firmly against your face so that impact with the water won't dislodge the mask, thereby breaking its airtight seal.

When you have your mask stabilized and held in position, insert the snorkel in your mouth. Take a deep breath and look straight ahead. Then, with your weight forward just as if you were starting for a walk, simply take one giant stride out over the water. Forget about the leg that stayed on the pool edge. It will follow you just as it always has.

The thing to strive for in the giant stride is to go no deeper in the water than you have to. The wider your stride, the less you will sink, especially if you begin bringing your fins together (generating *upwards* thrust) just after they become submerged.

One more front entry aid you can use when wearing snorkeling gear is to leave your left arm straight out at your side as you take the giant stride. As you hit the

1. To begin the back roll, sit on the pool edge and hold your mask.

2. As you fall backwards, your fins will start to rise.

3. Keep your hands on your mask until the entry is complete.

4. You'll probably end up doing a somersault, which is fine.

5. Note how the impact is almost completely on the back. For this reason, such a dive is never done from higher than a few feet.

water, bring the arm sharply down and this will also help keep you from going so deep. When you return to the top, blast clear the snorkel as soon as the top of your head breaks the surface.

Because you blew some air into your BC before entry, you should be quite positively buoyant after your entry. If you plan to make a dive right where you are, flutter your fins beneath you for upwards support, lift the BC hose and purge the air from your vest so that you can descend. If you intend to descend in another part of the pool, you might just leave the air in your vest until you've reached the spot. Or, you might even add more air for increased buoyancy on the way.

BACK ROLL ENTRY

The back roll is frequently used when making entry from the gunwale of a small boat. It gets you into the water without excessively rocking a craft. You can practice in the pool by doing this:

Sit down on the pool edge with your back to the water. Do all the things you did in the giant stride entry with your BC, mask, snorkel, etc., and just let yourself fall over

1. Kathy Cully shows the proper position for a slide-in entry.

2. The weight is shifted outwards, over the hands and pool edge.

3. The slide-in entry keeps you completely oriented and is the easiest to use of all the ones described.

backwards into the water. Your legs will automatically rise above you as you roll and you should strike the water at a point just below the shoulders. This dive is disorienting for a second or two, and should *never* be done from a height greater than a few feet.

OTHER ENTRIES

Several other entries can be made for special reasons such as getting to the bottom very quickly. Various feet-first entries and a headfirst roll technique are not discussed here because they can be dangerous to practice in a pool without instruction and, what's more, they are mainly of benefit when wearing scuba equipment. During your basic scuba certification course, your instructor will certainly show you the giant stride, back roll and possibly others for use in both scuba and skindiving. You'll also learn techniques for entering the ocean from a beach or over rocks, where you'll be concerned with currents, surf, selection of entrance and exit points along a coast or jetty, as well as dozens of other considerations about open water diving. Obviously, since these circumstances cannot be simulated in a pool, you'll have to learn them in the course without benefit of pool prepractice.

8
Surface
Dives

When you are snorkeling along the surface, you'll frequently want to descend to study a fish below. In order to avoid scaring the fish, it's best to make a quiet, sleek dive which avoids excessive splashing. Also, as a breath-holding snorkeler, you're very concerned with getting down fast so you can spend more time underwater. You'll learn two basic surface dives in your certification course. They are simple to learn, though seldom done well by beginners the first few times. Here are the dives and how you can practice each one.

SURFACE DIVE
(Jackknife)

VERTICAL DIVE
- FEET FOREMOST-
(Kelp Dive)

1. The jackknife surface dive begins anytime you want to descend quietly to the bottom.
2. To jackknife, lift your fins to the surface while you drop your head under water.
3. Keep your legs flat on the surface until you're pointed straight down as shown in this excellent jackknife dive by Barb Steiner.
4. Notice how a good jackknife dive barely disturbs the water.
5. The moment you're pointing straight towards the bottom, lift your legs as high out of the water as they'll go. Their weight pushes you quietly down.
6. Few fish would be disturbed by such a smoothly performed surface dive and graceful glide downwards.

1. *The starting position for a feet-first or "kelp" surface dive finds you with your arms and legs spread far apart. It's called a kelp dive because when you're in forests of kelp, you'd likely become entangled in leaves and strands if you were to do the jackknife dive shown earlier.*

2. *You gain upwards propulsion by simultaneously bringing your arms and legs together in one massive "stroke."*

3. *This massive stroke drives much of your body's weight well out of the water.*

Jackknife or Pike

Snorkel along the surface with your fins underwater and your BC deflated. When you reach a point above the drain in the pool, take a deep breath and bend at the waist until your body and arms are pointing straight down at the drain. Then lift your legs straight up, completely out of the water. The weight of your raised legs will force you down to the drain. For added velocity, sweep your arms back to your sides as you drop.

Always remember that the key to a successful headfirst surface dive lies in getting your torso pointed straight down and your feet and legs pointed straight up as quickly as possible. The higher your legs rise out of the water, the farther down you'll go.

Feet First "Kelp" Dive

Start this dive in deep pool water with your head above the surface and your body pointing straight down. Extend your arms wide at your sides and spread your legs far apart. Then bring your arms together at your sides just as

4. After rising, you hold your arms and legs together so your body's weight will push you straight down. Note that the entire dive takes place in a very small area so as to avoid kelp, weeds, or other objects at the surface.
5. Once you've driven yourself well under the surface and any entanglements there, you simply swim off to continue your dive.

your legs close in a powerful scissors kick. This thrust will carry you out of the water nearly to your waist.

Next, just let your rigid body slide straight down. When you stop descending, tuck your fins behind your seat, roll forward, and swim to the pool bottom or off to the side.

Practicing in a pool will help you when you enter a scuba diving course, but it won't qualify you for safe open-water diving. Only professional instruction will safely do that.

9
Review
of Precourse
Training

After you've completed the exercises given here, you will know the *basics only* of using, in a pool, the following pieces of gear: Buoyancy compensator, mask, snorkel, and fins. You'll have also learned the basics only of making a few pool entries, surface dives, and several kicks.

In short, you'll really know just enough to be dangerous to yourself and others in anything but a pool environment. *That's why you need professional instruction to polish your new skills, evaluate them and be absolutely sure they're really adequate for use in open water.*

Should You Take a Scuba Course?

If you decide to take a basic scuba certification course, this practice will put you well ahead of most of your classmates in proficiency. How far ahead depends entirely on how much you practice the exercises outlined in this book. Should you decide against taking a scuba certification course, you might at least take a basic course in snorkel diving. These are offered by many of the same national certifying organizations which teach scuba diving. The only difference in taking a snorkel diving course is that you'll not learn to scuba dive, thus not receive a scuba certification card. And without a C card, you cannot buy air at a dive store or on a charter dive boat.

The worst possible mistake you could ever make, based on your newly learned snorkeling skills, is to dive with scuba gear. This book purposely avoids extended discussion of scuba techniques in the hopes that you'll concentrate instead on learning the important basics, the proper use of BC, mask, snorkel, and fins. Master the fundamentals and your scuba diving course will likely be a breeze, providing you're both physically and mentally qualified. And providing you maintain that critical ability to be COMFORTABLE IN THE WATER.

Weighing Your "Margin of Safety"

One of the nation's most knowledgeable veteran scuba experts outlined for me his rules and guidelines for "smart" diving. He says, "Stop diving when you are tired or cold or have injured yourself in any way, or if you run out of air or are not having fun. If you become uncomfortable in the water—that is the time to terminate your dive and leave the water."

He also cautions that you should know your personal limits but never actually reach them. Instead, he advises that you leave yourself a "margin of safety" to cover any emergencies which might arise. Your limits, as explained by this diving veteran of twenty years, are determined largely by the length of time you've been in the water, the distance you've traveled, and your comfort level.

He adds that this margin of safety varies, even with the same person. It depends on how long it's been since the last dive, what was eaten for breakfast that morning, the amount of sleep the preceding night, how much hard exercise has been done recently, and many other factors. Most of all, it depends on taking time to think about such things *before* entering the water—or even deciding whether to go diving at all if conditions are not right.

To a great degree, an experienced diver has an advantage over a less experienced one, even if the novice is in slightly better physical condition. This is because the seasoned diver knows better how to pace himself, minimize extraneous motion, relax parts of his body not in use, and so on. In addition, his hard-earned ability to be always COMFORTABLE IN THE WATER means his heart and lung functions will be nearer to normal, and he will tire less easily.

How deep you go, how far, and how long you stay become a matter of weighing your *personal* margin of safety against an *honest* appraisal of your overall condition before *every* dive. When you begin ignoring this margin of safety, you become a counterfeit to both yourself, your buddy, and the entire community of a half-million active divers in this country. If you dive when you know you shouldn't, and have an injury or fatality, you could hurt not only yourself and your survivors but also the entire future of sport diving.

Your foolishness could bring on ill-conceived, unfair laws against a sport which has been maligned long enough by a few uninformed journalists with large readerships and some overzealous legislators whose powerful influence supersedes their well-meant but uninformed attempts to "protect participants in the sport of diving."

Those of us who love the underwater freedom of a new world welcome you if you're mature enough to first learn the rules and always play by them. When I spoke earlier about "diving's unique fraternity," I also meant it was unique in its discipline of those who don't follow the rules. This is not to say that if you exhibit foolhardy behavior before other divers, they will do you in 80 feet down. But chances are they'll never invite you to dive with them again unless you can somehow prove that you've started using your head.

10 Choosing Proper Instruction

The Need for Good Training

During your formal education, whether it was in the elementary grades, high school, or college, you found out there are some very excellent teachers and there are some who taught students with a mind simply to "crank them out."

You found out how a particularly concerned teacher could make an impact on you which has lasted your entire life. Whether it was a clever shortcut to solving specific kinds of mathematical problems, or a certain insight to finding happiness in dealing with yourself and others, chances are most of the things you remember well and use today to make your life easier were learned from someone who truly cared about you and your future.

In choosing a scuba instructor, you should look for one who really cares about what kind of a diver you'll become. This does not mean that your criteria for selection is simply to find a "nice" instructor, rather, find one who'll make sure you've *learned* all he's tried to teach you. Sometimes the most gruff instructor in your area is the best. He might have the reputation of being "tough," but this may simply be a reputation earned because he demanded more than just *minimum* standards of performance from his students.

The point is that while you want to choose a very good instructor, you can't judge that person from what he or she says to you or how he looks. The best criteria to use is this: a consensus of opinion from his past students who are now certified scuba divers. Before you can gain this information, however, you must first locate the subject whom you'll be investigating. The following steps will be of help in this process.

Locating Instructors.

Since there are only about 5,000 active scuba instructors in the country, finding one in your area may be a little difficult unless you contact firms or organizations which regularly deal with them. Once again, the best place to start is the yellow pages of the telephone book. Look under Diving, Divers' Supplies, Skin Diving, Scuba Instruction, and etc.

First, try calling retail diving stores in your area. Tell the person who answers the call that you're interested in taking a basic scuba course and ask for the date when the next complete course begins. Also, call your local YMCA, high schools, and colleges, as well as parks and recreation departments. Such institutions frequently offer scuba instruction. Ask for the name of the instructor who'll be teaching the course.

Shopping for a Course—10 Questions to Ask

As you make each call, write down the information received on a sheet of paper. At the top, list the organization's address and phone number and the name of the person with whom you spoke. Make a separate sheet for each place called if there are several in your area. On the same sheet of paper, note the answers received to the following questions:

1. How many total hours of instruction are included in the course?
2. How many of these hours are devoted to:
    (a) lecture sessions
    (b) pool training
    (c) open-water instruction
3. What certification is given?
4. Specifically, what is the cost of the *entire* certification course and precisely what does it include in the way of:
    (a) equipment rental
    (b) boat trips
    (c) text books
    (d) instructor's fee
    (e) charge for C card
    (f) charges for air tank fills
    (g) any additional charges
5. How many open-water dives are included?
    (a) beach dives
    (b) boat dives
6. What are the names and phone numbers of some

persons who have completed a course during the last six months from the same instructor I will have?

7. When and where may I attend a pool or lecture training segment of this instructor's course during the next few weeks?

8. How many weekends, evenings, days, and etc. does the course take to complete?

9. How many students are usually in each pool and open-water training under one instructor's supervision?

10. If I give you my name and address, will you send me the brochure which describes the basic scuba certification course you offer?

The reason you ask these questions of several places is to make sure you're not only receiving the best available instruction possible in your area but the best that can be had for the money. While it is quite rare, some instructors connected with dive stores and even a few independent ones have been known to pack a course with hidden costs or quote a course price which does not include all the costs you'll need to bear from start to finish.

A good example of this is a dive store instructor who says, "Yes sir, our basic scuba course is fifty dollars and that includes all the instruction, plus rental of mask, snorkel, fins, and BC."

Unfortunately, what he may not have told you was that when you begin using scuba gear during pool training, you must separately rent a tank, regulator, and backpack, each at several dollars a session over and above the $50 course charge. Also, he may have "forgotten" to mention that the two open water boat trips included in the course each carry a charter boat charge of $15, as well as additional rental charges for a weight belt, knife, wet suit, gauges, and who knows what else.

On the other hand, it is true that most dive stores and instructors have a stake in maintaining a good reputation for fair dealing because that is how they gain referral business. So chances are very good you'll be given a course price which includes every cost you'll incur from your first day of training to your last. Nevertheless, you may as well protect yourself from the few hucksters who somehow stay in business.

The answers to the questions you wrote down will tell you much about the quality and cost/value relationship of the course you'll ultimately choose. So your analysis can be thorough, the questions are given on the next page, followed by what you should consider for each one.

1. *How many total hours of instruction are included in the course?*

● The various national certifying groups vary in the total hours included in a basic scuba certification course. Therefore, a good basic course may run from 24 to 40 hours.

2. *How many of these hours are devoted to:*

		Hours
(a)	Lecture sessions	10-16
(b)	Pool training	12-16
(c)	Open-water instruction	2-8
	Total:	24-40

● Rate open-water instruction highest, then pool training, then finally lecture sessions.

3. *What certification is given?*

● Ideally, you'll prefer a nationally recognized certification so that you can be confident that thought went into carefully designing the course; you want to know that you can travel almost anywhere with assurance that your certification card will be honored by firms and groups which are bound by ethics, or in some cases by law, to refuse to put air into a dive cylinder unless the person requesting the air can present proof he is a certified diver.

For that reason, beware of locally issued certifications. It is safest to look for and accept only certifications from these *nationally* recognized organizations:

NASDS (National Association of Skin Diving Schools)
NAUI (National Association of Underwater Instructors)
PADI (Professional Association of Diving Instructors)
YMCA (Young Men's Christian Association)

4. *Specifically, what is the cost of the entire certification course and precisely what does it include in the way of:*

(a) *equipment rental*
(b) *boat trips*
(c) *text books*
(d) *instructors fees*
(e) *charge for C card*
(f) *charges for air tank fills*
(g) *any additional charges*

● What you want here is a ring of honesty in the voice of the person quoting prices. If you hear a lot of "Oh, yes, now that you mention it, there is an additional charge for X," then you might really probe for a no-nonsense, total course price. Also, make a notation on the sheet for that company that you felt you were perhaps being "conned" a bit. However, remember that there's usually a difference in the responses you'll receive from a dive store *salesman* and an instructor who's affiliated with a dive store. The former is in the business of selling you equipment (perhaps he's on a commission basis) while the latter should primarily be interested in having you join the fraternity of well-trained scuba divers.

Remember, too, that many instructors are also instructor/salesmen. But a good instructor/salesman is capable of separating his two roles into their proper perspectives. Just because he's connected with a profit-oriented retail dive store doesn't mean he's automatically out to "get you." If he views his dual role ethically, an instructor salesman may be of great advantage to you later in helping choose your equipment.

Beware, however, if he seems continually to favor one manufacturer's brand over all others. Should that happen, immediately confront him by asking if he gains a larger commission on the brand he keeps pushing or if it's the only major brand of equipment he carries.

5. *How many open-water dives are included?*
   (a) *beach dives*
   (b) *boat dives*
● Your course should offer a minimum of three open-water dives. If there are more, that's to your benefit. The course having more open-water dives may be higher in cost but, after all, you didn't intend a lifetime of sport diving in a pool anyway. So the more open-water instruction you can get in a course, the more confident you'll become and the more COMFORTABLE YOU'LL BE IN THE WATER.

In courses offering three open-water dives, geographic location and water availability usually dictate the number of dives taken from a beach or a boat. If you're hundreds of miles from an ocean, you can't easily experience the problems of swimming out through surf. Thus beach dives to you in a lake or quarry will be a snap. The often used standard among certifying organizations is as follows: at least one hour of open-water training is to be underwater, on scuba. One dive is to be a skin dive (snorkel dive) done from the shore. The other two dives may consist of one scuba dive done from the shore and one scuba dive done from boat or shore. No more than two scuba dives are to be credited in any one day, with no more than six hours of open-water training to be received in any one day.

6. *What are the names and phone numbers of some persons who have completed a course during the last six months from the same instructor I'll have?*
● This is one of the most important questions you can ask. If the organization is truly providing good instruc-

tion, they should have many students who are well satisfied with their training and the person teaching the course. Now it's possible you'll be given the names of students whom the organization believes will say nice things about the training. In view of this possibility, be sure you probe deeply with specific questions when phoning the former scuba students. The reason you ask for several names is that you'll probably only be able to reach one or two persons at the most, so it's better to have a *list* of names and numbers to call. Otherwise you might reach no one.

When you do contact a former student, don't simply ask "Was the instructor tough?" because that's irrelevant to your needs. Ask, instead, "Did the instructor seem to care how much you'd learned?" That's far more important. Also, be sure to ask the former students all the other questions about course content, price, number of open-water dives, and so on. In particular, find out whether they feel they got what they were promised, because that's what really helps you to make the best choice.

7. *When and where may I attend a pool or lecture training segment of this instructor's course during the next few weeks?*

● Since at this point you have no frame of reference for evaluating the quality of a training session, this visit may be somewhat experiential. Nonetheless, you'll get to talk to the *current* students, plus you'll meet the instructor and see some of what you'll be doing when you enter a scuba course. Beyond that, it shows the organization that you're serious enough about taking a course to make an extra effort. It also tells the same thing to the instructor—which could result in your receiving extra attention once your course begins. This can be of definite advantage, especially if you have initial problems mastering some aspect of your training.

8. *How many weekends, evenings, days, and etc. does the course take to complete?*

● Depending on your time availability, this is an important consideration. Training at a high school or college could run a few hours a day, every week, for sixteen weeks. Conversely, some courses run all day long on succeeding days, until completion. The majority of basic certification courses, however, are held twice a week over a period of three to six weeks. You'll have to determine the best sequence for your personal schedule.

9. *How many students are there usually in each pool session and open-water dive under one instructor's supervision?*

● Ideally, the ratio of students to instructor generally agreed upon by the national certifying organizations is twelve students per instructor during water work in a pool, confined, or protected water, or when skin diving in open water. The ratio should not exceed eight to one when using scuba in open water. Remember, too, in making your evaluation that these are *ideal* ratios. Sometimes conditions preclude hitting the exact numbers.

Assistant instructors are also sometimes used in certification courses. If conditions allow, the recommended ratio is one assistant for each four student divers during open-water scuba diving.

In lecture sessions, there may be a far greater ratio of students per instructor. That is fine, but always consider that your opportunity for personal attention and time for question-asking decreases as the lecture group size increases.

10. *If I give you my name and address, will you send me the brochure which describes the basic scuba certification course you offer?*

● You ask this question mainly to find out who has brochures and who doesn't. Typically, a stable, well-organized firm or group offering scuba instruction will have a *printed* brochure outlining specifics and costs of its course. Since printing is fairly expensive, you can bet they print their fliers in large quantities for economy, as well as changing the copy and art as infrequently as possible as an economy measure. Ideally, this means the instruction described in their brochure basically stays the same. This is to your advantage since the mere fact it's written down means you have a better chance of holding the firm to providing exactly what their brochure promised for exactly that price.

You might be a bit skeptical of firms or organizations who offer no brochure or other printed course description. Since they have nothing in writing, you can't easily hold them to a *verbal* promise of giving a certain amount of training or equipment usage for the fee.

In all fairness, however, instructors who are independent of institutions or retail firms seldom can afford to fund their own printed brochure. In such cases it's a good idea to have the instructor simply write down and sign a fairly complete outline description of what his course to you includes, plus all related costs.

Spending a few hours on the phone comparing course offerings can often mean the difference between gaining either adequate basic scuba instruction or exceptional instruction. The key is to find the best instructor in your area who offers the most comprehensive course for the money.

The author displays a large spider crab he captured off Catalina Island during his first dive after gaining his basic scuba certification.

11
Summary

The ultimate point of this book is to show you that you can probably qualify for a scuba course if you are both mentally and physically prepared for it.

The mental part is determined by you after honestly evaluating yourself. The physical part is determined by you after a qualified doctor says that you *can* scuba dive. Then simply get yourself in shape so you pass the course entry requirements. That's it. So you see, right now you are entirely in control of whether or not you'll ever become a certified scuba diver.

Forget all the "frightening" myths you've heard about sharks, diving fatalities, running out of air, superhuman strength, and the rest of the untruths. Quit *thinking* about scuba diving and just get started *doing* something about it.

And when you do get started, don't merely *try* to do what you want to do, because that's never enough for your success or your happiness at anything. Whenever you get started, don't *try* to do it—go out there and *do* it!

You get started doing something about scuba diving by following the steps outlined in this book. You can either read the book and put it down and go on *thinking* about diving or you can read it and then follow the step-by-step exercises. If you *do* the latter, you'll have stopped thinking about becoming a diver and will suddenly be well on your way to being one. Yes, you take a long conceptual step to move from a position of "thinking" and "trying" to "doing" and "being." And maybe that's why only one out of a hundred persons is a diver—because it requires you to commit yourself in such a hard way.

Anyone can buy a tennis racquet and some balls and start playing tennis. In diving, though, you must first prove yourself qualified to enjoy the sport. What that represents to you is a challenge to your self-esteem and to whatever else you think you might risk losing if you don't make it. That's part of the reason some people rationalize about diving to themselves and never get around to it. It's always far easier to avoid the experience completely than it is to experience the experience. Particularly when you think you have something to lose or hide. The truth is, however, that you have nothing to lose but the experience itself, and once it's gone it's just gone, and that's it. You're still where you were.

You're not around very long to do things like scuba dive or fly a plane or climb a mountain or swim a channel or even write a book. Each time you experience those challenges, however, you have made yourself a little more alive by causing yourself to come to grips with a challenge.

That's what the people on T.V. who sell beer are trying to tell you even though they really want you to buy their brand of beer. When they say, "Grab all the gusto you can," the "gusto" is experience. If you seek gusto in your life, you'll find it there every time you go scuba diving.

Appendix

MEDICAL EXAMINATION FORM

Please print or type

NAME _____ AGE _____ SEX _____

ADDRESS _____ CITY _____ ZIP _____

OCCUPATION _____ HOME PHONE _____

HEIGHT _____ inches WEIGHT _____ POUNDS

To The Physician:

This person is an applicant for training in diving with self-contained underwater breathing apparatus (SCUBA). This is an activity which puts unusual stress on the individual in several ways. Your opinion of the applicant's medical fitness is desired. Scuba diving requires heavy exertion. The diver must be free of cardiovascular and respiratory diseases. An absolute requirement is the ability of the middle ear and sinuses to equalize pressure. Any condition that risks the loss of consciousness should disqualify the applicant.

You will note that the medical examination form presents three (3) alternative choices under IMPRESSION. If you conclude that diving is not in the individual's best interest, please discuss your opinion with him frankly. If he persists in desiring to dive, and if definite threat to his life and health is NOT involved, CONDITIONAL APPROVAL may be indicated. This will be considered with the understanding that the applicant has been told why you do not consider him fully qualified and that he accepts the responsibility for going ahead with the program.

References of possible value to the physician conducting medical examinations for scuba diving:

CNCA, *New Science of Skin and Scuba Diving, 1968*
Dueker, *Medical Aspects of Sport Diving, 1970*
Miles, *Underwater Medicine, 1969*
USGPO, *U.S. Navy Diving Manual, 1970*

If there are any questions, please contact:

Instructor name, address, phone

Physician's Notes (see reverse side for medical history): _____

_____

_____

- - - - - - - - - - - - - - - - TEAR OFF HERE - - - - - - - - - - - - - - - -

Applicant's Name _____

IMPRESSION:

_____ 1. APPROVAL (I find no defects which I consider incompatible with diving.)

_____ 2. CONDITIONAL APPROVAL (I do not consider diving in this person's best interest but find no defects which present marked risk. I have discussed my impression with the patient.) Reason for conditional approval _____

_____

_____ 3. DISAPPROVAL (This applicant has defects which in my opinion clearly would constitute unacceptable hazards to his health and safety in diving.)

Date _____ Signature _____ , M.D.

Address _____ Phone _____

MEDICAL HISTORY FORM

Please print or type

Name _____

Before your medical examination by the physician, this entire side and the top of the reverse side should be completed. Be prepared to discuss any abnormalities or problems with your physician.

Check the appropriate blank if any of the following apply to you, and explain under remarks, indicating the item number.

___ 1. Previous diving experience	___ 13. Epilepsy	___ 24. Persistent cough
___ 2. Participate in active sports	___ 14. Heart trouble	___ 25. Breathing difficulty
___ 3. Electrocardiogram	___ 15. Frequent colds or sore throat	___ 26. Smoke or drink
___ 4. Trouble equalizing pressure	___ 16. Severe or frequent headaches	___ 27. Motion sickness
___ 5. Dizziness or fainting	___ 17. Rejected from any activity for medical reasons	___ 28. Claustrophobia
___ 6. Mental or emotional problems	___ 18. Ear trouble	___ 29. Nervous breakdown
___ 7. Recent operation or illness	___ 19. Hay fever	___ 30. Diabetes
___ 8. Hospitalized	___ 20. Asthma	___ 31. Glasses or contacts
___ 9. Serious injury	___ 21. Sinus trouble	___ 32. Hearing difficulty
___ 10. Physical handicap	___ 22. Tuberculosis	___ 33. Chest pain
___ 11. Regular medication	___ 23. Respiratory problems	___ 34. Any serious medical problem not listed
___ 12. Allergies, including drugs		

Remarks _____

_____

_____

_____

Date of previous medical examination _____   Date of chest X-ray _____

NOTE: Physician is to retain the upper portion of this form and the lower portion is to be returned by the applicant as the course application.

-------------------------------- TEAR OFF HERE --------------------------------

Legal Name (for certification or records) _____

Nickname (for informal course use) _____

Home Address _____ City _____ State _____ Zip _____

Birthdate _____ Age _____ Sex _____ Home Phone _____ City _____

Course applied for: _____

In case of an emergency, contact:

Name _____ Relationship _____ Phone _____

Doctor _____ Day Phone _____ Night Phone _____

Medical Insurance Co. _____ Policy No. _____ Phone _____

How did you learn of this course? _____

Index